Judges

K.W. Bow

Copyright 2017 by Kenneth W. Bow
The book author retains sole copyright to
his contributions to this book.
Published 2017.
Printed in the United States of America.

All rights reserved.

No portion of this book may be reproduced, stored in a retrieval system, or transmitted in any form or by any means – electronic, mechanical, photocopy, recording, scanning, or other – except for brief quotations in critical reviews or articles, without the prior written permission of the author.

ISBN 978-1-946234-10-0

Cover art and design: Mark Gauthier.
Editor-in-chief: Susan Lind.

This book was published by BookCrafters,
Parker, Colorado.
bookcrafterscolorado@gmail.com

This book may be ordered from
www.bookcrafters.net and other online bookstores.

Foreword

Thank you reader, for selecting my book. There are many choices of books and we all have a limited window of time to read. I appreciate you purchasing my product. It is a humbling thing to know someone would choose to purchase, and then read your work. I do not take it as a small matter. By purchasing and reading a book, the reader and the author form a certain bond as they travel a road together for a short time. It is especially rewarding when the two agree on the content. It is my hope you can find inspiration and life challenges in the pages of this small booklet.

From the days of my high school years I have found the Bible fascinating. I have travelled to Israel on two occasions to learn more about the land and culture of the Bible. I worked on an archaeological dig and lived on a Kibbutz to better inform myself of how to understand this book from God. I have read it from cover to cover over twenty times, and it is still as exciting to me as it ever was.

The Bible is a magnificent journey and experience. It is ever a delight. In it you will travel to distant lands and meet some of the most incredible people of history. It will introduce you to kings and peasants. You will walk the palace halls of castles and the open fields of the countryside. You will meet the famous and be introduced to people whose name we will never know. You will read some of the greatest love stories ever told and you will see the dark side of man as the evil manifests itself in heinous ways. Every emotion of man is highlighted at some time. You will see greed and avarice and murderous covetousness. You will also see the greatest examples of love and sacrifice that mankind has ever contributed. For indeed the Bible is the story of man. It is the whole story, and nothing is left out or omitted. It is the ultimate mirror of life.

When we invest time in the Bible we indulge a bit of the eternal. The Bible will never pass away, even in the eons of the future. If you have read it sincerely then my hope is this small work will intensify your understanding and enjoyment a little more. It is the grandest journey we can make while in this life. Thank you for sharing a portion of your life journey with me.

Kenneth Bow

Judges

The book of Judges opens to us one of the darkest times of man's history. The people of God should have been celebrating victories and conquering a new land. Judges opens the window into the heart of mankind, and the picture is not pretty.

Seven times in the book the statement is made "every man did that which was right in his own eyes." The result of that environment was catastrophic. It further emphasis that there was no King in those days. So every man was left to follow his own decisions.

This period of time lasted 450 years. This period of time was as long as the entire duration of the monarchy. Because there is one book of Judges, and six books of the Kings (Samuel, Kings, Chronicles), it is natural to feel like the Kings were a longer period of time. Both of these time periods were 450 years. Why?

God gave man 450 years to reveal what happens when man does that which is right in his own eyes. The result of that time period is so abhorrent and tragic, we scarce can comprehend it. The last five chapters of Judges are as bad and ugly as any period of history, any place on the globe. From this experiment and experience we can truly agree with God that it is not in man to direct his steps.

It might help to think of these Judges as freedom fighters. These judges were not perfect people, in fact some of them were badly flawed. They used methods that seemed unfair and even dishonest. The word Judge to us today speaks of courtrooms and juries. These men, (and one woman), were liberators, fighters, leaders of armies. They are renowned for their military campaigns. The following is a list of Judges and their term of time.

Judge	Enemy
Othniel/40 years	Mesopotamia
Ehud/80 years	Moab, Amon, Amalek
Deborah, Barak/40 years	Caanan
Gideon/40 years	Midian
Abimelech/3 years	
Toah/23 years	
Jair/22 years	
Jeptha/6 years	Ammon
Ibzaim/7 years	
Elon/10 years	
Samson/20 years	Philistines
Eli/40 years	Philistines
Samuel/20 years	Philistines

There were 111 years of oppression and 339 years of peace for a total of 450 years of the reign of the Judges. This is the same amount of years for the Kings. There was 120 years of the United Kingdom, 200 years of a divided Kingdom with Israel and Judah side by side, and an additional 135 years of Judah.

The conclusion is this, God gave man 450 years of man doing what he thought was right on his own. Then he gave man 450 years where a king ruled over his life. Both time periods ended in failure. Opening the door for the prophets and God's voice being the law of man and earth. The only successful government has proved to be when God himself rules over the affairs of men.

In the first 16 chapters of Judges, it is all about God's people being attacked from without. The enemy is from the outside. Then the last five chapters are the result when Israel turns upon herself and begins to carnage herself. The result is one of the most terrible times in all of history. Before it is over Israel will have killed more of her own that any of her attackers from the outside. If fact, she will have killed more of her own that all of the outside attacks combined over the entire 450 year period.

What a statement God leaves on the pages of the Bible about what happens when we forget who our real enemy is and begin to war on our brothers.

In the last five chapters, it begins with the introduction of Idolatry into Israel with the story of Micah and his graven images. The stage is set for idolatry and it takes a thousand years and a dispersion (Israel), and a captivity (Judah), to finally purge Israel of Idolatry.

The story moves on to the tribe of Dan. This tribe is not satisfied with their inheritance so they look for new territory. They journey east, then north, a total of about 144 miles to conquer Laish. They rename the city "Dan"(hence the term from Dan to Beersheba). This is not the inheritance God assigned to the tribe of Dan. This story lets us see the terrible result of what happens when you are not satisfied with your inheritance. The tribe of Dan is forever removed from the pages of the Bible. The only mention I find is one descendant worked on Solomon's temple. Dan is never mentioned again, never included anymore in the list of the tribes all the way to the book of Revelation.

What more would anyone need to illustrate the danger of not being satisfied with our inheritance?

The book of Judges then moves on to the story of the concubine. The woman was abused and finally dies. Her master cuts her into twelve pieces and sends a piece of the evidence to each tribe. The nation goes to war and the result is horrific. Israel loses 65,000 men in the final chapters of Judges, all because they had a piece of the evidence. The tribe of Benjamin is reduced to 400 men and almost obliterated. I believe they would have been wiped out if not for a future son of Benjamin that would literally change the world, Saul of Tarsus. God preserved the tribe for Israel's first king, and Christianity's first missionary.

The moral of the story is again so stark. It is so dangerous to go to war over a piece of the evidence.

Was all lost for humanity? Not at all. God in his infinite wisdom was letting man work through the slow process of human government to help man self discover for himself his need of God.

All was not lost, for even in this morass, at the bull's eye center of the greatest carnage were faithful people who held on to God. That is why Boaz steps onto the stage in the book of Ruth. There was in the days of the Judges, Ruth 1.1

Boaz's home was a short distance from the epicenter of the great battle and carnage of the final chapters of Judges. Boaz's life in the book of Ruth proves there are always people who remain true to God, even in the times of apostasy.

Author: Anonymous

Chronology: 1400BC

Jesus in the book: The Captain of our salvation

Apostolic Themes: Victory, Conquest, Leadership

Chapter 1

1.1-4 Now after the death of Joshua it came to pass, that the children of Israel asked the Lord, saying, Who shall go up for us against the Canaanites first, to fight against them? 2 And the Lord said, Judah shall go up: behold, I have delivered the land into his hand. 3 And Judah said unto Simeon his brother, Come up with me into my lot, that we may fight against the Canaanites; and I likewise will go with thee into thy lot. So Simeon went with him. 4 And Judah went up; and the Lord delivered the Canaanites and the Perizzites into their hand: and they slew of them in Bezek ten thousand men.

1.1-4 The book of Judges continues from the book of Joshua. New issues were created by the death of Joshua. Since the Exodus, Israel had only had two leaders, Moses and Joshua. Now they were facing immense challenges without the leadership that had brought them this far. The people inquire of the Lord who to send up and God does not name a man, but rather a tribe. The ad infinitum mind of God transitions to the moment where the tribes replace the individual leader overseeing the new nation. This moment is critical. As with so many transitions in the Bible and in world history, there are no trumpets sounding. There are no announcements. It simply unfolds like a blooming rose in a garden. A golden age can never be pinpointed as to when it began, but can always be assessed when it begins its decline. The next 450 years are transitioned almost without notice except for this brief notice at the opening of this book. Leadership is passed from an individual to a tribal responsibility. This ushers in the era of every man doing that which is right in his own eyes. In the greater picture of God's plan for man on planet earth, this is significant. When the final judgment of man occurs at the end of time, God will have proven through all these eras He is just in His pronounced judgments. Judah and Simeon join forces to augment their strength. Here is the first tremor of this concept of every man doing what he thinks is right. God said Judah, God did not say Judah and Simeon. The slide has begun and will continue for 450 years.

1.5-8 And they found Adonibezek in Bezek: and they fought against him, and they slew the Canaanites and the Perizzites. 6 But Adonibezek fled; and they pursued after him, and caught him, and cut off his thumbs and his great toes. 7 And Adonibezek said, Threescore and ten kings, having their thumbs and their great toes cut off, gathered their meat under my table: as I have done, so God hath requited me. And they brought him to Jerusalem, and there he died. 8 Now the children of Judah had fought against Jerusalem, and had taken it, and smitten it with the edge of the sword, and set the city on fire.

1.5-8 Adonibezek. Here we see the concept of *lex talionis*, proportionate retribution. This is also called poetic justice. This wicked King has the same thing done to him that he has done to others. David proclaimed this principle in 2 Sam 22.27. With the froward God shows himself froward.

God answers our lives by how we dispense to others. Jesus continues this theme in His sermon on the mount, with what judgment you judge, ye shall be judged (Mt 7.1).

1.9-15 And afterward the children of Judah went down to fight against the Canaanites, that dwelt in the mountain, and in the south, and in the valley. 10 And Judah went against the Canaanites that dwelt in Hebron: (now the name of Hebron before was Kirjatharba:) and they slew Sheshai, and Ahiman, and Talmai. 11 And from thence he went against the inhabitants of Debir: and the name of Debir before was Kirjathsepher: 12 And Caleb said, He that smiteth Kirjathsepher, and taketh it, to him will I give Achsah my daughter to wife. 13 And Othniel the son of Kenaz, Caleb's younger brother, took it: and he gave him Achsah his daughter to wife. 14 And it came to pass, when she came to him, that she moved him to ask of her father a field: and she lighted from off her ass; and Caleb said unto her, What wilt thou? 15 And she said unto him, Give me a blessing: for thou hast given me a south land; give me also springs of water. And Caleb gave her the upper springs and the nether springs.

1.9-15 The city of Debir had been taken in an earlier campaign (Joshua 10.38). This was evidently a recapture. This was done by Caleb's nephew and son-in-law, Othniel. Othniel becomes the first Judge. We see here the flexibility of the inheritance with Caleb's daughter Achsah. Caleb concedes her request for the land and the upper springs.

1.16-26 And the children of the Kenite, Moses' father in law, went up out of the city of palm trees with the

children of Judah into the wilderness of Judah, which lieth in the south of Arad; and they went and dwelt among the people. 17 And Judah went with Simeon his brother, and they slew the Canaanites that inhabited Zephath, and utterly destroyed it. And the name of the city was called Hormah. 18 Also Judah took Gaza with the coast thereof, and Askelon with the coast thereof, and Ekron with the coast thereof. 19 And the Lord was with Judah; and he drave out the inhabitants of the mountain; but could not drive out the inhabitants of the valley, because they had chariots of iron. 20 And they gave Hebron unto Caleb, as Moses said: and he expelled thence the three sons of Anak. 21 And the children of Benjamin did not drive out the Jebusites that inhabited Jerusalem; but the Jebusites dwell with the children of Benjamin in Jerusalem unto this day. 22 And the house of Joseph, they also went up against Bethel: and the Lord was with them. 23 And the house of Joseph sent to descry Bethel. (Now the name of the city before was Luz.) 24 And the spies saw a man come forth out of the city, and they said unto him, Shew us, we pray thee, the entrance into the city, and we will shew thee mercy. 25 And when he shewed them the entrance into the city, they smote the city with the edge of the sword; but they let go the man and all his family. 26 And the man went into the land of the Hittites, and built a city, and called the name thereof Luz: which is the name thereof unto this day.

1.16-26 Judah's war. The list of conquered cities is, Zephath, Gaza, Ekron. By contrast Benjamin and Joseph are not successful in their wars. The inhabitants of the land had chariots of iron and this proves to be a hindrance in conquering the land. God helped them at times as the story of the conquest of Bethel illustrates.

1.27-36 Neither did Manasseh drive out the inhabitants of Bethshean and her towns, nor Taanach and her towns, nor the inhabitants of Dor and her towns, nor the inhabitants of Ibleam and her towns, nor the inhabitants of Megiddo and her towns: but the Canaanites would dwell in that land. 28 And it came to pass, when Israel was strong, that they put the Canaanites to tribute, and did not utterly drive them out. 29 Neither did Ephraim drive out the Canaanites that dwelt in Gezer; but the Canaanites dwelt in Gezer among them. 30 Neither did Zebulun drive out the inhabitants of Kitron, nor the inhabitants of Nahalol; but the Canaanites dwelt among them, and became tributaries. 31 Neither did Asher drive out the inhabitants of Accho, nor the inhabitants of Zidon, nor of Ahlab, nor of Achzib, nor of Helbah, nor of Aphik, nor of Rehob: 32 But the Asherites dwelt among the Canaanites, the inhabitants of the land: for they did not drive them out. 33 Neither did Naphtali drive out the inhabitants of Bethshemesh, nor the inhabitants of Bethanath; but he dwelt among the Canaanites, the inhabitants of the land: nevertheless the inhabitants of Bethshemesh and of Bethanath became tributaries unto them. 34 And the Amorites forced the children of Dan into the mountain: for they would not suffer them to come down to the valley: 35 But the Amorites would dwell in mount Heres in Aijalon, and in Shaalbim: yet the hand of the house of Joseph prevailed, so that they became tributaries. 36 And the coast of the Amorites was from the going up to Akrabbim, from the rock, and upward.

1.27-36 The failure. Manasseh, Ephraim, Zebulun, Asher, Naphtali, and Dan all failed to complete their conquests. The majority of these tribes allowed their adversaries to live among them as tributaries. Even though there may have been circumstances that made total conquest difficult, the scriptures state this is a spiritual failure. The next chapter makes it abundantly clear God is not pleased. The period of time when man did what was right in his own eyes is already bearing the fruits of failure.

Chapter 2

2.1-5 And an angel of the Lord came up from Gilgal to Bochim, and said, I made you to go up out of Egypt, and have brought you unto the land which I sware unto your fathers; and I said, I will never break my covenant with you. 2 And ye shall make no league with the inhabitants of this land; ye shall throw down their altars: but ye have not obeyed my voice: why have ye done this? 3 Wherefore I also said, I will not drive them out from before you; but they shall be as thorns in your sides, and their gods shall be a snare unto you. 4 And it came to pass, when the angel of the Lord spake these words unto all the children of Israel, that the people lifted up their voice, and wept. 5 And they called the name of that place Bochim: and they sacrificed there unto the Lord.

2.1-5 God tries. God always tries. He tries to gently push man in the right direction. The issues from the garden of Eden prevail, and self will asserts itself repeatedly. God sends an angel to rebuke and instruct. The journey of the angel reflects their journey also. Gilgal was such an important moment in their history. It was there that their curse of the wilderness was rolled away. The signal from God is return to your commitments to follow me. They are reminded to cast out the inhabitants of the land and destroy their altars. Upon hearing the angel, the people wept, and named the place Bochim (weepers).

2.6-10 And when Joshua had let the people go, the children of Israel went every man unto his inheritance to possess the land. 7 And the people served the Lord all the days of Joshua, and all the days of the elders that outlived Joshua, who had seen all the great works of the Lord, that he did for Israel. 8 And Joshua the son of Nun, the servant of the Lord, died, being an hundred and ten years old. 9 And they buried him in the border of his inheritance in Timnathheres, in the mount of Ephraim, on the north side of the hill Gaash. 10 And also all that generation were gathered unto their fathers: and there arose another generation after them, which knew not the Lord, nor yet the works which he had done for Israel.

2.6-10 Death of Joshua. The key to Joshua's greatness is seen in the appellation "the servant of the Lord." If Joshua had lived longer, the entire rubric of this narrative would be different. As it is, the God directed conduct of the nation lasted one more generation. The seed of self rule had now grown into a full blown tree and the fruit was terminal.

2.11-15 And the children of Israel did evil in the sight of the Lord, and served Baalim: 12 And they forsook the Lord God of their fathers, which brought them out of the land of Egypt, and followed other gods, of the gods of the people that were round about them, and bowed themselves unto them, and provoked the Lord to anger. 13 And they forsook the Lord, and served Baal and Ashtaroth. 14 And the anger of the Lord was hot against Israel, and he delivered them into the hands of spoilers that spoiled them, and he sold them into the hands of their enemies round about, so that they could not any longer stand before their enemies. 15 Whithersoever they went out, the hand of the Lord was against them for evil, as the Lord had said, and as the Lord had sworn unto them: and they were greatly distressed.

2.11-15 Baal. Their religion quickly becomes a travesty in the eyes of God. They turn to Baal. Baal was the chief deity of Canaan. He was a storm God that also bequeathed fertility. It is a sad epitaph on Israel that she so quickly adopted this worship and continued for so long. The Old Testament is replete with warnings against worshipping other Gods. Israel quickly falls into this rut and stays there for a thousand years.

2.16-23 Nevertheless the Lord raised up judges, which delivered them out of the hand of those that spoiled them. 17 And yet they would not hearken unto their judges, but they went a whoring after other gods, and bowed themselves unto them: they turned quickly out of the way which their fathers walked in, obeying the commandments of the Lord; but they did not so. 18 And when the Lord raised them up judges, then the Lord was with the judge, and delivered them out of the hand of their enemies all the days of the judge: for it repented the Lord because of their groanings by reason of them that oppressed them and vexed them. 19 And it came to pass, when the judge was dead, that they returned, and corrupted themselves more than their fathers, in following other gods to serve them, and to bow down unto them; they ceased not from their own doings, nor from their stubborn way. 20 And the anger of the Lord was hot against Israel; and he said, Because that this people hath transgressed my covenant which I commanded their fathers, and have not hearkened unto my voice; 21 I also will not henceforth drive out any from before them

of the nations which Joshua left when he died: 22 That through them I may prove Israel, whether they will keep the way of the Lord to walk therein, as their fathers did keep it, or not. 23 Therefore the Lord left those nations, without driving them out hastily; neither delivered he them into the hand of Joshua.

2.16-23 Judges. This passage succinctly explains the Judges. It is a roller coaster ride for 450 years. Every corner and part of the nation is affected. No region on the compass holds true to God. The book now begins to document region by region what happens when men do that which is right in their own eyes. This is the most graphic display in the history of mankind of the need of God. Man at his best is still at his lowest without God. The interludes of God raised, and God anointed freedom fighters to throw off the yoke of oppression, is stark, poignant and powerful. During the life of the judge, Israel thrived and conquered. At the death of the judge, the baseness of man bubbled to the top again and the cycle repeats. Each cycle seemed to take the populace a little lower. God decides to leave the opposing inhabitants of the land and use them to prove Israel. This proving was not for God for he knows the end from the beginning. This proving was for Israel to look into the mirror and see what happens when man is left to do what he thinks is right. Man without God is the most ugly sight of all. The next 19 chapters show that image in all its horror and shame. It is an image of repeated immorality, spiritual apostasy, and unmitigated failure.

Chapter 3

3.1-2 Now these are the nations which the Lord left, to prove Israel by them, even as many of Israel as had not known all the wars of Canaan; 2 Only that the generations of the children of Israel might know, to teach them war, at the least such as before knew nothing thereof;

3.1-2 Nations. The nations left unconquered in the Promised Land became a training module for Israel to learn the art of war. God uses bad and disappointing situations to create good things in our lives. All things work together for good (Rom 8.28). Not everything that happens to us is good, but God can bring something good from the worst of events.

3.3-6 Namely, five lords of the Philistines, and all the Canaanites, and the Sidonians, and the Hivites that dwelt in mount Lebanon, from mount Baalhermon unto the entering in of Hamath. 4 And they were to prove Israel by them, to know whether they would hearken unto the commandments of the Lord, which he commanded their fathers by the hand of Moses. 5 And the children of Israel dwelt among the Canaanites, Hittites, and Amorites, and Perizzites, and Hivites, and Jebusites: 6 And they took their daughters to be their wives, and gave their daughters to their sons, and served their gods.

3.3-6 Early failure. The fruit of every man doing what he felt was right continues to bear immediate and disastrous fruit. Israel began to serve the Gods of the land they were attempting to conquer and began to intermarry their children with the children of these heathen nations. Moses had warned of this in Ex 34 and again in Dt 7.

3.7-11 And the children of Israel did evil in the sight of the Lord, and forgat the Lord their God, and served Baalim and the groves. 8 Therefore the anger of the Lord was hot against Israel, and he sold them into the hand of Chushanrishathaim king of Mesopotamia: and the children of Israel served Chushanrishathaim eight years. 9 And when the children of Israel cried unto the Lord, the Lord raised up a deliverer to the children of Israel, who delivered them, even Othniel the son of Kenaz, Caleb's younger brother. 10 And the Spirit of the Lord came upon him, and he judged Israel, and went out to war: and the Lord delivered Chushanrishathaim king of Mesopotamia into his hand; and his hand prevailed against Chushanrishathaim. 11 And the land had rest forty years. And Othniel the son of Kenaz died.

3.7-11 Othniel. The son-in-law to Caleb was the first freedom fighter to rise up and war against the encroaching false religions. He witnessed this chosen nation forsake God and turn to Baal and the groves. Othniel bore the anger of God for eight years. Finally, the people cried unto God and God responded with deliverance. The land had rest forty years. Is there a significance of the forty years? This is the same length of time spent in the wilderness. Othniel was selected by God to be the first Judge; he was not selected by popular acclaim. God chose each of the 13 liberators Himself. There is no instance of choice by popularity or even ability. It was a sovereign choice by God.

3.12-30 And the children of Israel did evil again in the sight of the Lord: and the Lord strengthened Eglon the king of Moab against Israel, because they had done evil in the sight of the Lord. 13 And he gathered unto him the children of Ammon and Amalek, and went and smote Israel, and possessed the city of palm trees. 14 So the children of Israel served Eglon the king of Moab eighteen years. 15 But when the children of Israel cried unto the Lord, the Lord raised them up a deliverer, Ehud the son of Gera, a Benjamite, a man lefthanded: and by him the children of Israel sent a present unto Eglon the king of Moab. 16 But Ehud made him a dagger which had two edges, of a cubit length; and he did gird it under his raiment upon his right thigh. 17 And he brought the present unto Eglon king of Moab: and Eglon was a very fat man. 18 And when he had made an end to offer the present, he sent away the people that bare the present. 19 But he himself turned again from the quarries that were by Gilgal, and said, I have a secret errand unto thee, O king: who said, Keep silence. And all that stood by him went out from him. 20 And Ehud came unto him; and he was sitting in a summer parlour, which he had for himself alone. And Ehud said, I have a message from God unto thee. And he arose out of his seat. 21 And Ehud put forth his left hand, and took the dagger from his right thigh, and thrust it into his belly: 22 And the haft also went in after the blade; and the fat closed upon the blade, so that he could not draw the dagger out of his belly; and the dirt came out. 23 Then Ehud went forth through the porch, and shut the doors of the parlour upon him, and locked them. 24 When he was gone out, his servants came; and when they saw that, behold, the doors of the parlour were locked, they said, Surely he covereth his feet in his summer chamber. 25 And they tarried till they were ashamed: and, behold, he opened not the doors of the parlour; therefore they took a key, and opened them: and, behold, their lord was fallen down dead on the earth. 26 And Ehud escaped while they tarried, and passed beyond the quarries, and escaped unto Seirath. 27 And it came to pass, when he was come, that he blew a trumpet in the mountain of Ephraim, and the children of Israel went down with him from the mount, and he before them. 28 And he said unto them, Follow after me: for the Lord hath delivered your enemies the Moabites into your hand. And they went down after him, and took the fords of Jordan toward Moab, and suffered not a man to pass over. 29 And they slew of Moab at that time about ten thousand men, all lusty, and all men of valour; and there escaped not a man. 30 So Moab was subdued that day under the hand of Israel. And the land had rest fourscore years.

3.12-30 Ehud. Israel does evil again. What a pregnant little word, again is. The Hebrew word is *yasaph* and means to continue. The 40 years in the desert did not cure them and neither did the 40 years under Othniel. The spotlight moves to Ehud whom the scripture points out is left handed. This innocuous point would not have meaning if it only meant his left hand was his dominant hand. There is cause to believe his right hand was not functional either from birth or injury. Early on God wants to illustrate He uses the weak things of the world to confound the wise. The children of Israel had now been under abuse from Moab for 18 years. Ehud uses a dagger that specifically had two edges so to cut in both directions, thereby off setting the loss of the right hand. Ehud brings a present, a gift, a tribute offering to Eglon, the wicked King of Moab. Ehud knew that Eglon was a fat man and it would take a long dagger to reach Eglon's vital and kill him, so Ehud made his dagger a cubits length (18 inches). It appears Ehud sent the people home and when he reached the quarries where the stone idols were hewed, he reversed his course and returned to the mission he had planned. Eglon is in a summer parlor, which is a second story room or a rooftop used to view his domain. As they stand admiring the view and the countryside, Ehud does a cross draw with his left hand. His right side would never be suspected because of his faulty right hand. As the blade slides easily into his hand Ehud thrusts it all the way in to the haft of the home made dagger. Ehud knows he has pierced the vitals because the dirt (entrails) comes out. Ehud leaves quietly and locks the door and the servants assume Eglon is sleeping. Ehud literally single handedly brings down what an army would have struggled to achieve. Ehud blows the trumpet and the call to war is answered. 10,000 men of Moab are slain and Moab is subdued. This time the Lord gives the land 80 years of rest to prove to Israel their sinful nature will not die. The desire to do what their own heart wants may lay dormant for years, but eventually it asserts itself again.

3.31 And after him was Shamgar the son of Anath, which slew of the Philistines six hundred men with an ox goad: and he also delivered Israel.

3.31 Shamgar. Nineteen verses are devoted to Ehud. One verse to Shamgar. Shamgar slew six hundred men with an ox goad and delivered Israel. What is the cause of such brevity here? Why such detail about Ehud and such economy toward Shamgar? Added to his conciseness in mention is also the fact he is not called a judge. More importantly there is no mention of a time element as a result of this deliverance. Even more telling is that the narrative dates the next time stamp as the death of Ehud without a mention of Shamgar. The most appealing answer is that Ehud was in the Eastern part of Israel, while Shamgar was in the Western sector. This would infer Shamgar's years were included either in the 80 years of Ehud or the years of Deborah and Barak. The Hebrew word *achar* for after can also mean, beside. This lends toward the time of Shamgar being concurrent with Ehud.

Chapter 4

4.1-9 And the children of Israel again did evil in the sight of the Lord, when Ehud was dead. 2 And the Lord sold them into the hand of Jabin king of Canaan, that reigned in Hazor; the captain of whose host was Sisera, which dwelt in Harosheth of the Gentiles. 3 And the children of Israel cried unto the Lord: for he had nine hundred chariots of iron; and twenty years he mightily oppressed the children of Israel. 4 And Deborah, a prophetess, the wife of Lapidoth, she judged Israel at that time. 5 And she dwelt under the palm tree of Deborah between Ramah and Bethel in mount Ephraim: and the children of Israel came up to her for judgment. 6 And she sent and called Barak the son of Abinoam out of Kedeshnaphtali, and said unto him, Hath not the Lord God of Israel commanded, saying, Go and draw toward mount Tabor, and take with thee ten thousand men of the children of Naphtali and of the children of Zebulun? 7 And I will draw unto thee to the river Kishon Sisera, the captain of Jabin's army, with his chariots and his multitude; and I will deliver him into thine hand. 8 And Barak said unto her, If thou wilt go with me, then I will go: but if thou wilt not go with me, then I will not go. 9 And she said, I will surely go with thee: notwithstanding the journey that thou takest shall not be for thine honour; for the

Lord shall sell Sisera into the hand of a woman. And Deborah arose, and went with Barak to Kedesh.

4.1-9 Deborah (the northern region). We are now privy to know the office of a judge was more than military leadership. This is the third period of oppression and occurs in the 13th century BC. This is an important military victory because the Canaanite forces under the leadership of Sisera were superior. Sisera had 900 chariots of iron. This was a strategic battle for the control of central and Northern Palestine. After being oppressed for 20 years, Israel was experiencing longer and longer periods of foreign rule. Deborah was one of four women in the Old Testament identified as a prophetess. She is the only female Judge. Critics of the era of the Bible assert the Bible is unfair to women. This is a prime example of women holding key positions of power. She is joined by Jael, another woman, in this crucial victory. Chapter four gives the account of the battle and the details, while chapter 5 gives the song of victory. Barak's part in the battle is not to be over looked, for he is mentioned in the heroes of faith in Hebrews 11.32.

4.10-24 And Barak called Zebulun and Naphtali to Kedesh; and he went up with ten thousand men at his feet: and Deborah went up with him. 11 Now Heber the Kenite, which was of the children of Hobab the father in law of Moses, had severed himself from the Kenites, and pitched his tent unto the plain of Zaanaim, which is by Kedesh. 12 And they shewed Sisera that Barak the son of Abinoam was gone up to mount Tabor. 13 And Sisera gathered together all his chariots, even nine hundred chariots of iron, and all the people that were with him, from Harosheth of the Gentiles unto the river of Kishon. 14 And Deborah said unto Barak, Up; for this is the

day in which the Lord hath delivered Sisera into thine hand: is not the Lord gone out before thee? So Barak went down from mount Tabor, and ten thousand men after him. 15 And the Lord discomfited Sisera, and all his chariots, and all his host, with the edge of the sword before Barak; so that Sisera lighted down off his chariot, and fled away on his feet. 16 But Barak pursued after the chariots, and after the host, unto Harosheth of the Gentiles: and all the host of Sisera fell upon the edge of the sword; and there was not a man left. 17 Howbeit Sisera fled away on his feet to the tent of Jael the wife of Heber the Kenite: for there was peace between Jabin the king of Hazor and the house of Heber the Kenite. 18 And Jael went out to meet Sisera, and said unto him, Turn in, my lord, turn in to me; fear not. And when he had turned in unto her into the tent, she covered him with a mantle. 19 And he said unto her, Give me, I pray thee, a little water to drink; for I am thirsty. And she opened a bottle of milk, and gave him drink, and covered him. 20 Again he said unto her, Stand in the door of the tent, and it shall be, when any man doth come and enquire of thee, and say, Is there any man here? that thou shalt say, No. 21 Then Jael Heber's wife took a nail of the tent, and took an hammer in her hand, and went softly unto him, and smote the nail into his temples, and fastened it into the ground: for he was fast asleep and weary. So he died. 22 And, behold, as Barak pursued Sisera, Jael came out to meet him, and said unto him, Come, and I will shew thee the man whom thou seekest. And when he came into her tent, behold, Sisera lay dead, and the nail was in his temples. 23 So God subdued on that day Jabin the king of Canaan before the children of Israel. 24 And the hand of the children of Israel prospered, and prevailed against Jabin the king of Canaan, until they had destroyed Jabin king of Canaan.

4.10-24 The call of Zebulun and Naphtali. Before the battle is concluded men from six tribes will participate. Naphtali, Zebulun, Ephraim, Benjamin, Manasseh, and Issachar all participate. The directing of the battle given by Deborah in this critical encounter places her in the most favorable light of all of the judges. She is called a mother in Israel. The faith of Barak is fanned into flame by the spirit of this great woman. From the flat land tops of Tabor, Deborah and Barak watched the troops of Sisera assemble on the slopes of Carmel. It is at that moment that Deborah summons Barak to arise. She proclaims, "up; for this is the day in which the Lord hath delivered Sisera into thine hand." The Lord had already began his approach to battle with Sisera, Barak had only to follow in the wake of divine power. The book of Judges has now covered battles in the east under Ehud, in the west under Shamgar, and now the north and central under Deborah and Barak.

Chapter 5

5.1-3 Then sang Deborah and Barak the son of Abinoam on that day, saying, 2 Praise ye the Lord for the avenging of Israel, when the people willingly offered themselves. 3 Hear, O ye kings; give ear, O ye princes; I, even I, will sing unto the Lord; I will sing praise to the Lord God of Israel.

5.1-3 The Song of Deborah. This chapter is a poetic song of the battle in chapter 4. The avenging of Israel is a Hebrew phrase that is difficult to translate. It is about people who volunteer and willingly and spontaneously give of themselves freely.

5.4-10 Lord, when thou wentest out of Seir, when thou marchedst out of the field of Edom, the earth trembled, and the heavens dropped, the clouds also dropped water. 5 The mountains melted from before the Lord, even that Sinai from before the Lord God of Israel. 6 In the days of Shamgar the son of Anath, in the days of Jael, the highways were unoccupied, and the travellers walked through byways. 7 The inhabitants of the villages ceased, they ceased in Israel, until that I Deborah arose, that I arose a mother in Israel. 8 They chose new gods; then was war in the gates: was there a shield or spear seen among forty thousand in Israel? 9 My heart is toward the governors of Israel, that offered themselves willingly among the people. Bless ye the Lord. 10 Speak, ye that ride on white asses, ye that sit in judgment, and walk by the way.

5.4-10 Deborah sings to Kings to announce the greatness of the victory, and also serve notice this victory was of God. She recounts the event leading up to the great victory during the days of Shamgar and Jael. To all who ride on white asses (royalty), be advised God fights for Israel.

5.11-13 They that are delivered from the noise of archers in the places of drawing water, there shall they rehearse the righteous acts of the Lord, even the righteous acts toward the inhabitants of his villages in Israel: then shall the people of the Lord go down to the gates. 12 Awake, awake, Deborah: awake, awake, utter a song: arise, Barak, and lead thy captivity captive, thou son of Abinoam. 13 Then he made him that remaineth have dominion over the nobles among the people: the Lord made me have dominion over the mighty.

5.11-13 Awake. This admonition repeated twice for emphasis means to open the eyes. Israel had been spiritually asleep and the prophetess calls for a national awakening. This is one of the prominent roles of all prophets in the Bible. To awaken those who have fallen asleep. Then the call is to arise. The call to act follows the call to awake. To awake and not act is pointless. This is echoed in the New Testament in relation to faith. James declares faith without works is dead. Faith in Jesus Christ is just an awakening. Obeying the New Testament plan of salvation is action. This principal is always true in God's economy and is illustrated many times by Jesus and the Apostles. Our actions do not save us but our faith is of no effect unless we act.

5.14-18 Out of Ephraim was there a root of them against Amalek; after thee, Benjamin, among thy people; out of Machir came down governors, and out of Zebulun they that handle the pen of the writer. 15 And the princes of Issachar were with Deborah; even Issachar, and also Barak: he was sent on foot into the valley. For the divisions of Reuben there were great thoughts of heart. 16 Why abodest thou among the sheepfolds, to hear the bleatings of the flocks? For the divisions of Reuben there were great searchings of heart. 17 Gilead abode beyond Jordan: and why did Dan remain in ships? Asher continued on the sea shore, and abode in his breaches. 18 Zebulun and Naphtali were a people that jeoparded their lives unto the death in the high places of the field.

5.14-18 The accolades of the battles are now bestowed upon the tribes who fought. One trait of God is He never forgets to reward His servants. Deborah also chides the tribes who looked on without coming to aid in the battle. The prophet's role is to reward and to admonish.

5.19-24 The kings came and fought, then fought the kings of Canaan in Taanach by the waters of Megiddo; they took no gain of money. 20 They fought from heaven; the stars in their courses fought against Sisera. 21 The river of Kishon swept them away, that ancient river, the river Kishon. O my soul, thou hast trodden down strength. 22 Then were the horsehoofs broken by the means of the pransings, the pransings of their mighty ones. 23 Curse ye Meroz, said the angel of the Lord, curse ye bitterly the inhabitants thereof; because

they came not to the help of the Lord, to the help of the Lord against the mighty. 24 Blessed above women shall Jael the wife of Heber the Kenite be, blessed shall she be above women in the tent.

5.19-24 The kings. All the advantages of the heathen kings were nullified by God. God took away their advantages. Isaiah would say seven centuries later that no weapon formed against you shall prosper. The strength of the Canaanite's army became their arrearage.

5.25-27 He asked water, and she gave him milk; she brought forth butter in a lordly dish. 26 She put her hand to the nail, and her right hand to the workmen's hammer; and with the hammer she smote Sisera, she smote off his head, when she had pierced and stricken through his temples. 27 At her feet he bowed, he fell, he lay down: at her feet he bowed, he fell: where he bowed, there he fell down dead.

5.25-27 The song adds a detail that the report of battle leaves out. Jael cut off Sisera's head after she drove the tent stake through his head. This practice was not unusual in the Bible: example David and Goliath.

5.28-31 The mother of Sisera looked out at a window, and cried through the lattice, Why is his chariot so long in coming? why tarry the wheels of his chariots? 29 Her wise ladies answered her, yea, she returned answer to herself, 30 Have they not sped? have they not divided the prey; to every man a damsel or two; to Sisera a prey of divers colours, a prey of divers colours of needlework, of divers colours of needlework on both sides, meet for the necks of them that take the spoil? 31 So let all thine enemies perish, O Lord: but let them that love him be as

the sun when he goeth forth in his might. And the land had rest forty years.

5.28-31 With a nod of the head to the mother of Sisera as one woman to another, Deborah stays true to her purpose as a prophetess. This type of song would be common among the cultures of this era of time. Many countries have such odes to commemorate epic victories. The difference here is, God chose to have this song entered into the eternal record. While other ballads will fade in the morning glory of the dawn of eternity, The Song of Deborah shall ever be sung throughout the ages, a tribute to God and to those who willingly gave themselves.

Chapter 6

6.1-2 And the children of Israel did evil in the sight of the Lord: and the Lord delivered them into the hand of Midian seven years. 2 And the hand of Midian prevailed against Israel: and because of the Midianites the children of Israel made them the dens which are in the mountains, and caves, and strong holds.

6.1-2 Midian. The nation known as Midian was a descendant of Abraham and Keturah. This people had been sent away to the east so Isaac would have the land without strife. Joseph was sold by merchants from Midian. Moses fled to the land of Midian and married Zipporah. Midian joined Moab and Ammon to impede the progress of Israel to the promised land. Midianites were known as traders and usually associated with the Ishmaelites.

6.3-10 And so it was, when Israel had sown, that the Midianites came up, and the Amalekites, and the children of the east, even they came up against them; 4 And they encamped against them, and destroyed the increase of the earth, till thou come unto Gaza, and left no sustenance for Israel, neither sheep, nor ox, nor ass. 5 For they came up with their cattle and their tents, and they came as grasshoppers for multitude; for both

they and their camels were without number: and they entered into the land to destroy it. 6 And Israel was greatly impoverished because of the Midianites; and the children of Israel cried unto the Lord. 7 And it came to pass, when the children of Israel cried unto the Lord because of the Midianites, 8 That the Lord sent a prophet unto the children of Israel, which said unto them, Thus saith the Lord God of Israel, I brought you up from Egypt, and brought you forth out of the house of bondage; 9 And I delivered you out of the hand of the Egyptians, and out of the hand of all that oppressed you, and drave them out from before you, and gave you their land; 10 And I said unto you, I am the Lord your God; fear not the gods of the Amorites, in whose land ye dwell: but ye have not obeyed my voice.

6.3-10 Midian came to destroy the crops of Israel. There is no indication if there was warfare as well. The Midianites did not steal the crops, they simply destroyed them to starve Israel.

6.11-27 And there came an angel of the Lord, and sat under an oak which was in Ophrah, that pertained unto Joash the Abiezrite: and his son Gideon threshed wheat by the winepress, to hide it from the Midianites. 12 And the angel of the Lord appeared unto him, and said unto him, The Lord is with thee, thou mighty man of valour. 13 And Gideon said unto him, Oh my Lord, if the Lord be with us, why then is all this befallen us? and where be all his miracles which our fathers told us of, saying, Did not the Lord bring us up from Egypt? but now the Lord hath forsaken us, and delivered us into the hands of the Midianites. 14 And the Lord looked upon him, and said, Go in this thy might, and thou shalt save Israel from the hand of the Midianites: have not I sent thee? 15

And he said unto him, Oh my Lord, wherewith shall I save Israel? behold, my family is poor in Manasseh, and I am the least in my father's house. 16 And the Lord said unto him, Surely I will be with thee, and thou shalt smite the Midianites as one man. 17 And he said unto him, If now I have found grace in thy sight, then shew me a sign that thou talkest with me. 18 Depart not hence, I pray thee, until I come unto thee, and bring forth my present, and set it before thee. And he said, I will tarry until thou come again. 19 And Gideon went in, and made ready a kid, and unleavened cakes of an ephah of flour: the flesh he put in a basket, and he put the broth in a pot, and brought it out unto him under the oak, and presented it. 20 And the angel of God said unto him, Take the flesh and the unleavened cakes, and lay them upon this rock, and pour out the broth. And he did so. 21 Then the angel of the Lord put forth the end of the staff that was in his hand, and touched the flesh and the unleavened cakes; and there rose up fire out of the rock, and consumed the flesh and the unleavened cakes. Then the angel of the Lord departed out of his sight. 22 And when Gideon perceived that he was an angel of the Lord, Gideon said, Alas, O Lord God! for because I have seen an angel of the Lord face to face. 23 And the Lord said unto him, Peace be unto thee; fear not: thou shalt not die. 24 Then Gideon built an altar there unto the Lord, and called it Jehovahshalom: unto this day it is yet in Ophrah of the Abiezrites. 25 And it came to pass the same night, that the Lord said unto him, Take thy father's young bullock, even the second bullock of seven years old, and throw down the altar of Baal that thy father hath, and cut down the grove that is by it: 26 And build an altar unto the Lord thy God upon the top of this rock, in the ordered place, and take the second bullock, and offer a burnt sacrifice with the wood of the grove which thou shalt cut down. 27 Then Gideon took ten men of his servants, and did as the Lord had said unto him: and so it was, because he feared his father's household, and the men of the city, that he could not do it by day, that he did it by night.

6.11-27 Gideon (central region). This is one of the best known characters of the scriptures. The script provides plot, counter plot and entertainment. Israel had been impoverished for 7 years. An angel appears to Gideon and deems him a mighty man of valour. The reposte here is classic God verses man. This ageless dialog has been argued for millenniums. God always patiently wades through men's objections and denials. Gideon takes this classic dialog one step further and requires proof. God could easily have jettisoned Gideon at this point and chose another, but as He has with many others, God is patient with man's unbelief. Gideon is put to the test of obedience. He is told to destroy his father's altar built to Baal. Out of fear, Gideon prefers to do the deed under cover of darkness. He repeats this tendency to operate under the cover of darkness when he fights the army of Midian.

6.28-35 And when the men of the city arose early in the morning, behold, the altar of Baal was cast down, and the grove was cut down that was by it, and the second bullock was offered upon the altar that was built. 29 And they said one to another, Who hath done this thing? And when they enquired and asked, they said, Gideon the son of Joash hath done this thing. 30 Then the men of the city said unto Joash, Bring out thy son, that he may die: because he hath cast down the altar of Baal, and because he hath cut down the grove that was by it. 31 And Joash said unto all that stood against him, Will ye plead for Baal? will ye save him? he that will plead for him, let him be put to death whilst it is yet morning:

if he be a god, let him plead for himself, because one hath cast down his altar. 32 Therefore on that day he called him Jerubbaal, saying, Let Baal plead against him, because he hath thrown down his altar. 33 Then all the Midianites and the Amalekites and the children of the east were gathered together, and went over, and pitched in the valley of Jezreel. 34 But the Spirit of the Lord came upon Gideon, and he blew a trumpet; and Abiezer was gathered after him. 35 And he sent messengers throughout all Manasseh; who also was gathered after him: and he sent messengers unto Asher, and unto Zebulun, and unto Naphtali; and they came up to meet them.

6.28-35 By destroying the altar of Baal, the men fear the loss of what few crops are left that have not been destroyed by Midian. Baal was the weather God and they needed rain. When Gideon is charged he faces being executed. This is no small crime for their families were starving. Gideon's father defends his son and challenges them to let the God Baal defend himself. They bestow upon Gideon the name of Jerbubaal, which means Baal will contend. Midian and Amalek gather in the valley of Jezreel to rape the country of Israel once again. The stage is being set for one of the most dramatic events in the Bible.

6.36-40 And Gideon said unto God, If thou wilt save Israel by mine hand, as thou hast said, 37 Behold, I will put a fleece of wool in the floor; and if the dew be on the fleece only, and it be dry upon all the earth beside, then shall I know that thou wilt save Israel by mine hand, as thou hast said. 38 And it was so: for he rose up early on the morrow, and thrust the fleece together, and wringed the dew out of the fleece, a bowl full of water. 39 And Gideon said unto God, Let not thine anger be hot against

me, and I will speak but this once: let me prove, I pray thee, but this once with the fleece; let it now be dry only upon the fleece, and upon all the ground let there be dew. 40 And God did so that night: for it was dry upon the fleece only, and there was dew on all the ground.

6.36-40 The fleece. This is also one of the most well known moments of the Bible. People today still call a test they place before God a fleece, meaning they want God to confirm which direction they should go, or what decision is the one God wants. Gideon is unique in that he places the test and then after God answers, he reverses the test and asks again. The patience of God is amazing, God shows no recrimination toward Gideon.

Chapter 7

7.1-8 Then Jerubbaal, who is Gideon, and all the people that were with him, rose up early, and pitched beside the well of Harod: so that the host of the Midianites were on the north side of them, by the hill of Moreh, in the valley. 2 And the Lord said unto Gideon, The people that are with thee are too many for me to give the Midianites into their hands, lest Israel vaunt themselves against me, saying, Mine own hand hath saved me. 3 Now therefore go to, proclaim in the ears of the people, saying, Whosoever is fearful and afraid, let him return and depart early from mount Gilead. And there returned of the people twenty and two thousand; and there remained ten thousand. 4 And the Lord said unto Gideon, The people are yet too many; bring them down unto the water, and I will try them for thee there: and it shall be, that of whom I say unto thee, This shall go with thee, the same shall go with thee; and of whomsoever I say unto thee, This shall not go with thee, the same shall not go. 5 So he brought down the people unto the water: and the Lord said unto Gideon, Every one that lappeth of the water with his tongue, as a dog lappeth, him shalt thou set by himself; likewise every one that boweth down upon his knees to drink. 6 And the number of them that lapped, putting their hand to their mouth, were three hundred men:

but all the rest of the people bowed down upon their knees to drink water. 7 And the Lord said unto Gideon, By the three hundred men that lapped will I save you, and deliver the Midianites into thine hand: and let all the other people go every man unto his place. 8 So the people took victuals in their hand, and their trumpets: and he sent all the rest of Israel every man unto his tent, and retained those three hundred men: and the host of Midian was beneath him in the valley.

7.1-8 Quantity verses quality. Ps 33.16 There is no king saved by the multitude of an host. The concept of dismissing those who are fearful is Biblical. Dt 20.8 sets this precedent. Fear is infectious. Fear causes you to look at the enemy rather than looking at God. Fear can cause the faith of others to waiver. 22,000 go home because they are infected with fear. The next selection process involved practical wisdom to be alert to battle conditions, this eliminated another 10,000. Gideon is left with 300 men to rout 135,000. The world has never seen a stranger mobilization policy. Gideon would use surprise and confusion as tactics of war. This was a divinely inspired plan from God. Other times God gave unusual directives and the war was won by atypical methods (2 Chr 20.22-23).

7.9-15 And it came to pass the same night, that the Lord said unto him, Arise, get thee down unto the host; for I have delivered it into thine hand. 10 But if thou fear to go down, go thou with Phurah thy servant down to the host: 11 And thou shalt hear what they say; and afterward shall thine hands be strengthened to go down unto the host. Then went he down with Phurah his servant unto the outside of the armed men that were in the host. 12 And the Midianites and the Amalekites and all the children of the east lay along in the valley like grasshoppers for multitude; and their camels were without number, as the sand by the sea side for multitude. 13 And when Gideon was come, behold, there was a man that told a dream unto his fellow, and said, Behold, I dreamed a dream, and, lo, a cake of barley bread tumbled into the host of Midian, and came unto a tent, and smote it that it fell, and overturned it, that the tent lay along. 14 And his fellow answered and said, This is nothing else save the sword of Gideon the son of Joash, a man of Israel: for into his hand hath God delivered Midian, and all the host. 15 And it was so, when Gideon heard the telling of the dream, and the interpretation thereof, that he worshipped, and returned into the host of Israel, and said, Arise; for the Lord hath delivered into your hand the host of Midian.

7.9-15 The barley loaf. God gives Gideon reassurance in the form of a dream of the enemy. It involves the barley loaf, which is the most common kind of bread. The symbolism of this common, inexpensive loaf destroying a tent registered with Gideon and ignited his faith. Gideon saw this as a symbol of his weakness and an auspice of victory. The enemy in the tent confirmed this in Gideon's hearing giving Gideon even more confirmation.

7.16-18 And he divided the three hundred men into three companies, and he put a trumpet in every man's hand, with empty pitchers, and lamps within the pitchers. 17 And he said unto them, Look on me, and do likewise: and, behold, when I come to the outside of the camp, it shall be that, as I do, so shall ye do. 18 When I blow with a trumpet, I and all that are with me, then blow ye the trumpets also on every side of all the camp, and say, The sword of the Lord, and of Gideon.

7.16-18 The plan. We must wonder what the soldiers with Gideon thought when he revealed his battle plan. The three columns of men surround the enemy camp and follow the lead of Gideon. They shout the sword of the Lord and of Gideon. They have no physical sword, yet they shout they do. They include Gideon with the shout, for God uses men to do His bidding. God partners with the weak and base things of the world to show His glory. This divine plan worked to perfection. The sword of Midian became the sword of the Lord to execute victory.

7.19-25 So Gideon, and the hundred men that were with him, came unto the outside of the camp in the beginning of the middle watch; and they had but newly set the watch: and they blew the trumpets, and brake the pitchers that were in their hands. 20 And the three companies blew the trumpets, and brake the pitchers, and held the lamps in their left hands, and the trumpets in their right hands to blow withal: and they cried, The sword of the Lord, and of Gideon. 21 And they stood every man in his place round about the camp; and all the host ran, and cried, and fled. 22 And the three hundred blew the trumpets, and the Lord set every man's sword against his fellow, even throughout all the host: and the host fled to Bethshittah in Zererath, and to the border of Abelmeholah, unto Tabbath. 23 And the men of Israel gathered themselves together out of Naphtali, and out of Asher, and out of all Manasseh, and pursued after the Midianites. 24 And Gideon sent messengers throughout all mount Ephraim, saying, come down against the Midianites, and take before them the waters unto Bethbarah and Jordan. Then all the men of Ephraim gathered themselves together, and took the waters unto Bethbarah and Jordan. 25 And they took two princes of the Midianites, Oreb and Zeeb; and

they slew Oreb upon the rock Oreb, and Zeeb they slew at the winepress of Zeeb, and pursued Midian, and brought the heads of Oreb and Zeeb to Gideon on the other side Jordan.

7.19-25 Ephraim. The battle was successful, and the enemy was routed. Now the narrative turns to the mopping up phase of the campaign. Gideon counted on the Ephraimites to cut off the remnants that were escaping. This also was successful and two kings of Midian are slain.

Chapter 8

8.1-3 And the men of Ephraim said unto him, Why hast thou served us thus, that thou calledst us not, when thou wentest to fight with the Midianites? And they did chide with him sharply. 2 And he said unto them, What have I done now in comparison of you? Is not the gleaning of the grapes of Ephraim better than the vintage of Abiezer? 3 God hath delivered into your hands the princes of Midian, Oreb and Zeeb: and what was I able to do in comparison of you? Then their anger was abated toward him, when he had said that.

8.1-3 The anger of Ephraim. When the Ephraimites met Gideon they were angry with Gideon for not including them in the original battle. This is injured ambition. Ephraim wanted the exalted position of having won the victory. Gideon shows humility. He acknowledges their great contribution as more valuable than his own. God also mentions this great victory in Is 10.26.

8.4-21 And Gideon came to Jordan, and passed over, he, and the three hundred men that were with him, faint, yet pursuing them. 5 And he said unto the men of Succoth, Give, I pray you, loaves of bread unto the people that follow me; for they be faint, and I am

pursuing after Zebah and Zalmunna, kings of Midian. 6 And the princes of Succoth said, Are the hands of Zebah and Zalmunna now in thine hand, that we should give bread unto thine army? 7 And Gideon said, Therefore when the Lord hath delivered Zebah and Zalmunna into mine hand, then I will tear your flesh with the thorns of the wilderness and with briers. 8 And he went up thence to Penuel, and spake unto them likewise: and the men of Penuel answered him as the men of Succoth had answered him. 9 And he spake also unto the men of Penuel, saying, When I come again in peace, I will break down this tower. 10 Now Zebah and Zalmunna were in Karkor, and their hosts with them, about fifteen thousand men, all that were left of all the hosts of the children of the east: for there fell an hundred and twenty thousand men that drew sword. 11 And Gideon went up by the way of them that dwelt in tents on the east of Nobah and Jogbehah, and smote the host; for the host was secure. 12 And when Zebah and Zalmunna fled, he pursued after them, and took the two kings of Midian, Zebah and Zalmunna, and discomfited all the host. 13 And Gideon the son of Joash returned from battle before the sun was up, 14 And caught a young man of the men of Succoth, and enquired of him: and he described unto him the princes of Succoth, and the elders thereof, even threescore and seventeen men. 15 And he came unto the men of Succoth, and said, Behold Zebah and Zalmunna, with whom ye did upbraid me, saying, Are the hands of Zebah and Zalmunna now in thine hand, that we should give bread unto thy men that are weary? 16 And he took the elders of the city, and thorns of the wilderness and briers, and with them he taught the men of Succoth. 17 And he beat down the tower of Penuel, and slew the men of the city. 18 Then said he unto Zebah and Zalmunna, What manner of men were they whom ye slew at Tabor?

And they answered, As thou art, so were they; each one resembled the children of a king. 19 And he said, They were my brethren, even the sons of my mother: as the Lord liveth, if ye had saved them alive, I would not slay you. 20 And he said unto Jether his firstborn, Up, and slay them. But the youth drew not his sword: for he feared, because he was yet a youth. 21 Then Zebah and Zalmunna said, Rise thou, and fall upon us: for as the man is, so is his strength. And Gideon arose, and slew Zebah and Zalmunna, and took away the ornaments that were on their camels' necks.

8.4-21 The residents of various towns mentioned here were reluctant to help Gideon. This is because they feared retribution from Midian if Gideon's victory proved inconclusive. The reaction of Gideon is similar to that of Jesus many centuries later. Jesus said he that is not with me is against me, Mt 12.30. The resulting judgment on those who will not align themselves with a righteous cause is again a New Testament principal. The concluding part of Jesus great sermon in Matthew 25 deals with this concept. God takes it personal. He says, ye did it unto me. A large part of our eternal judgment is meted out by whose side we chose to be on. Middle ground is no option in God's world.

8.22-27 Then the men of Israel said unto Gideon, Rule thou over us, both thou, and thy son, and thy son's son also: for thou hast delivered us from the hand of Midian. 23 And Gideon said unto them, I will not rule over you, neither shall my son rule over you: the Lord shall rule over you. 24 And Gideon said unto them, I would desire a request of you, that ye would give me every man the earrings of his prey. (For they had golden earrings, because they were Ishmaelites.) 25 And they answered,

We will willingly give them. And they spread a garment, and did cast therein every man the earrings of his prey. 26 And the weight of the golden earrings that he requested was a thousand and seven hundred shekels of gold; beside ornaments, and collars, and purple raiment that was on the kings of Midian, and beside the chains that were about their camels' necks. 27 And Gideon made an ephod thereof, and put it in his city, even in Ophrah: and all Israel went thither a whoring after it: which thing became a snare unto Gideon, and to his house.

8.22-27 Gideon's ephod. This is an unusual part of the narrative. Gideon refuses to be exalted in the eyes of the people and tries to direct their religious loyalty toward an object of God. So much about this is noble and praiseworthy. The people take this well intentioned object and worship it, rather than God himself. This proclivity of man redounds throughout history. The worship of an image of things made by man has entrapped millions of people. This is the foundation of most man made religion and was the purpose of the commandment to not make any graven image. God saw the heart of man and put a commandment to protect man from himself. Gideon's ephod became the opposite of its intended purpose and led people into idolatry.

8.28-35 Thus was Midian subdued before the children of Israel, so that they lifted up their heads no more. And the country was in quietness forty years in the days of Gideon. 29 And Jerubbaal the son of Joash went and dwelt in his own house. 30 And Gideon had threescore and ten sons of his body begotten: for he had many wives. 31 And his concubine that was in Shechem, she also bare him a son, whose name he called Abimelech. 32 And Gideon the son of Joash died in a good old age, and was buried in the sepulchre of Joash his father, in Ophrah of the Abiezrites. **33 And it came to pass, as soon as Gideon was dead, that the children of Israel turned again, and went a whoring after Baalim, and made Baalberith their god. 34 And the children of Israel remembered not the Lord their God, who had delivered them out of the hands of all their enemies on every side: 35 Neither shewed they kindness to the house of Jerubbaal, namely, Gideon, according to all the goodness which he had shewed unto Israel.**

8.28-35 As the sun sets on the season of Gideon, 40 years of peace ensue. The life of the greatest Abiezrite in Israel's history is concluded. His influence was powerful, for as soon as he died, all Israel turns again to idolatry. The power of a leader is seen here. One man kept hundreds of thousands from idolatry. Israel not only forgets God, but also forgets Gideon the great judge from the family of Abiezer. Such is the nature of fallen humanity.

Chapter 9

9.1-5 And Abimelech the son of Jerubbaal went to Shechem unto his mother's brethren, and communed with them, and with all the family of the house of his mother's father, saying, 2 Speak, I pray you, in the ears of all the men of Shechem, Whether is better for you, either that all the sons of Jerubbaal, which are threescore and ten persons, reign over you, or that one reign over you? remember also that I am your bone and your flesh. 3 And his mother's brethren spake of him in the ears of all the men of Shechem all these words: and their hearts inclined to follow Abimelech; for they said, He is our brother. 4 And they gave him threescore and ten pieces of silver out of the house of Baalberith, wherewith Abimelech hired vain and light persons, which followed him. 5 And he went unto his father's house at Ophrah, and slew his brethren the sons of Jerubbaal, being threescore and ten persons, upon one stone: notwithstanding yet Jotham the youngest son of Jerubbaal was left; for he hid himself.

9.1-5 Abimelech. Abimelech was the King of Shechem during the time of the judges. He was Gideon's son by a concubine. He reigned 3 years in Shechem. He killed the 70 sons of Gideon in hopes of being the ruler of Israel also. The youngest son, Jotham was not killed.

9.6-21 And all the men of Shechem gathered together, and all the house of Millo, and went, and made Abimelech king, by the plain of the pillar that was in Shechem. 7 And when they told it to Jotham, he went and stood in the top of mount Gerizim, and lifted up his voice, and cried, and said unto them, Hearken unto me, ye men of Shechem, that God may hearken unto you. 8 The trees went forth on a time to anoint a king over them; and they said unto the olive tree, Reign thou over us. 9 But the olive tree said unto them, Should I leave my fatness, wherewith by me they honour God and man, and go to be promoted over the trees? 10 And the trees said to the fig tree, Come thou, and reign over us. 11 But the fig tree said unto them, Should I forsake my sweetness, and my good fruit, and go to be promoted over the trees? 12 Then said the trees unto the vine, Come thou, and reign over us. 13 And the vine said unto them, Should I leave my wine, which cheereth God and man, and go to be promoted over the trees? 14 Then said all the trees unto the bramble, Come thou, and reign over us. 15 And the bramble said unto the trees, If in truth ye anoint me king over you, then come and put your trust in my shadow: and if not, let fire come out of the bramble, and devour the cedars of Lebanon. 16 Now therefore, if ye have done truly and sincerely, in that ye have made Abimelech king, and if ye have dealt well with Jerubbaal and his house, and have done unto him according to the deserving of his hands; 17 (For my father fought for you, and adventured his life far, and delivered you out of the hand of Midian: 18 And ye are risen up against my father's house this day, and have slain his sons, threescore and ten persons, upon one stone, and have made Abimelech, the son of his maidservant, king over the men of Shechem, because he is your brother;) 19 If ye then have dealt truly and sincerely with Jerubbaal and with his house this day, then rejoice ye in Abimelech, and let him also rejoice in you: 20 But if not, let fire come out from Abimelech, and devour the men of Shechem, and the house of Millo; and let fire come out from the men of Shechem, and from the house of Millo, and devour Abimelech. 21 And Jotham ran away, and fled, and went to Beer, and dwelt there, for fear of Abimelech his brother.

9.6-21 Abimelech is made king of Shechem. He is called out by Gideon's youngest son Jotham. The parable Jotham puts forth is about trees. Jotham likens Abimelech to a bramble, inferring he is not even a tree. He is not a legitimate tree. Jotham then runs for his life fearing the retribution of Abimelech. Jotham declares they have brought on their own destruction.

9.22-57 When Abimelech had reigned three years over Israel, 23 Then God sent an evil spirit between Abimelech and the men of Shechem; and the men of Shechem dealt treacherously with Abimelech: 24 That the cruelty done to the threescore and ten sons of Jerubbaal might come, and their blood be laid upon Abimelech their brother, which slew them; and upon the men of Shechem, which aided him in the killing of his brethren. 25 And the men of Shechem set liers in wait for him in the top of the mountains, and they robbed all that came along that way by them: and it was told Abimelech. 26 And Gaal the son of Ebed came with his brethren, and went over to Shechem: and the men of Shechem put their confidence in him. 27 And they went out into the fields, and gathered their vineyards, and trode the grapes, and made merry, and went into the house of their god, and did eat and drink, and cursed Abimelech. 28 And Gaal the son of Ebed said, Who is Abimelech, and who is Shechem, that we should serve him? is not he the son of Jerubbaal? and

Zebul his officer? serve the men of Hamor the father of Shechem: for why should we serve him? 29 And would to God this people were under my hand! then would I remove Abimelech. And he said to Abimelech, Increase thine army, and come out. 30 And when Zebul the ruler of the city heard the words of Gaal the son of Ebed, his anger was kindled. 31 And he sent messengers unto Abimelech privily, saying, Behold, Gaal the son of Ebed and his brethren be come to Shechem; and, behold, they fortify the city against thee. 32 Now therefore up by night, thou and the people that is with thee, and lie in wait in the field: 33 And it shall be, that in the morning, as soon as the sun is up, thou shalt rise early, and set upon the city: and, behold, when he and the people that is with him come out against thee, then mayest thou do to them as thou shalt find occasion. 34 And Abimelech rose up, and all the people that were with him, by night, and they laid wait against Shechem in four companies. 35 And Gaal the son of Ebed went out, and stood in the entering of the gate of the city: and Abimelech rose up, and the people that were with him, from lying in wait. 36 And when Gaal saw the people, he said to Zebul, Behold, there come people down from the top of the mountains. And Zebul said unto him, Thou seest the shadow of the mountains as if they were men. 37 And Gaal spake again, and said, See there come people down by the middle of the land, and another company come along by the plain of Meonenim. 38 Then said Zebul unto him, Where is now thy mouth, wherewith thou saidst, Who is Abimelech, that we should serve him? is not this the people that thou hast despised? go out, I pray now, and fight with them. 39 And Gaal went out before the men of Shechem, and fought with Abimelech. 40 And Abimelech chased him, and he fled before him, and many were overthrown and wounded, even unto the entering of the gate. 41 And Abimelech dwelt at Arumah: and Zebul thrust out Gaal and his brethren, that they should not dwell in Shechem. 42 And it came to pass on the morrow, that the people went out into the field; and they told Abimelech. 43 And he took the people, and divided them into three companies, and laid wait in the field, and looked, and, behold, the people were come forth out of the city; and he rose up against them, and smote them. 44 And Abimelech, and the company that was with him, rushed forward, and stood in the entering of the gate of the city: and the two other companies ran upon all the people that were in the fields, and slew them. 45 And Abimelech fought against the city all that day; and he took the city, and slew the people that was therein, and beat down the city, and sowed it with salt. 46 And when all the men of the tower of Shechem heard that, they entered into an hold of the house of the god Berith. 47 And it was told Abimelech, that all the men of the tower of Shechem were gathered together. 48 And Abimelech gat him up to mount Zalmon, he and all the people that were with him; and Abimelech took an axe in his hand, and cut down a bough from the trees, and took it, and laid it on his shoulder, and said unto the people that were with him, What ye have seen me do, make haste, and do as I have done. 49 And all the people likewise cut down every man his bough, and followed Abimelech, and put them to the hold, and set the hold on fire upon them; so that all the men of the tower of Shechem died also, about a thousand men and women. 50 Then went Abimelech to Thebez, and encamped against Thebez, and took it. 51 But there was a strong tower within the city, and thither fled all the men and women, and all they of the city, and shut it to them, and gat them up to the top of the tower. 52 And Abimelech came unto the tower, and fought against it, and went hard unto the door of the tower to burn it with fire. 53 And a certain woman cast a piece of a millstone upon Abimelech's head, and all to brake his skull. 54 Then he called hastily unto the young man his armourbearer, and said unto him, Draw thy sword, and slay me, that men say not of me, A women slew him. And his young man thrust him through, and he died. 55 And when the men of Israel saw that Abimelech was dead, they departed every man unto his place. 56 Thus God rendered the wickedness of Abimelech, which he did unto his father, in slaying his seventy brethren: 57 And all the evil of the men of Shechem did God render upon their heads: and upon them came the curse of Jotham the son of Jerubbaal.

9.22-57 The fall of Abimelech. After 3 years God sends an evil spirit between Abimelech and the men of Shechem. Abimelech shows us the difference between a king and a despot. Abimelech was reaping the consequences of his cruelty to the 70 sons of Gideon. Ps 7.15-17, Abimelech dug a pit and fell in it, his violent dealing came down on him. Finally Abimelech is killed in a battle where he goes too close to a wall and a woman drops a stone on his head. Jotham's fable comes to pass. Gaal, the son of Ebed seems to be a mercenary that the men of Shechem collude with. During the feast of the wine harvest, Gaal calls for a revolt against Abimelech. This anger against Abimelech may go back to his being the son of Gideon who destroyed the altar of Baal. War ensues between Gaal and Abimelech, and Gaal is defeated and humiliated. Abimelech continues his cruel ways by burning down the tower of Shechem with the men inside. Finally Abimelech is killed and God renders Abimelech's wickedness back on him. The question we face is why such detail about this man and few details about others? What are the criteria to cause a story like this to be detailed? The affairs of men do not seem to be something God necessarily documents for the Holy Record. The bigger picture here is the demise of Baal worship under Gideon and then the reinstatement of Baal worship under Abimelech. This theme does indeed merit attention to detail and for this reason we have the abundance of minutiae. This worship of Baal would continue to plague the nation of Israel for the next thousand years, and would only be cured by the Babylonian captivity.

Chapter 10

10.1-5 And after Abimelech there arose to defend Israel Tola the son of Puah, the son of Dodo, a man of Issachar; and he dwelt in Shamir in mount Ephraim. 2 And he judged Israel twenty and three years, and died, and was buried in Shamir. 3 And after him arose Jair, a Gileadite, and judged Israel twenty and two years. 4 And he had thirty sons that rode on thirty ass colts, and they had thirty cities, which are called Havothjair unto this day, which are in the land of Gilead. 5 And Jair died, and was buried in Camon.

10.1-5 Tolo and Jair. These two judges are classified as "minor" judges along with Shamgar, Izban, Elon and Abdon. They are considered thus because they have no record of military deliverance from oppressors. Their mention is brief. If the regional concept of the Book of Judges holds true, these enter the pages of Holy Record because of the region they occupy. They are from the eastern part of the nation. They are the defendants of Manasseh and the area of their rule is the inheritance of the tribe of Manasseh.

10.6-18 And the children of Israel did evil again in the sight of the Lord, and served Baalim, and Ashtaroth,

and the gods of Syria, and the gods of Zidon, and the gods of Moab, and the gods of the children of Ammon, and the gods of the Philistines, and forsook the Lord, and served not him. 7 And the anger of the Lord was hot against Israel, and he sold them into the hands of the Philistines, and into the hands of the children of Ammon. 8 And that year they vexed and oppressed the children of Israel: eighteen years, all the children of Israel that were on the other side Jordan in the land of the Amorites, which is in Gilead. 9 Moreover the children of Ammon passed over Jordan to fight also against Judah, and against Benjamin, and against the house of Ephraim; so that Israel was sore distressed. 10 And the children of Israel cried unto the Lord, saying, We have sinned against thee, both because we have forsaken our God, and also served Baalim. 11 And the Lord said unto the children of Israel, Did not I deliver you from the Egyptians, and from the Amorites, from the children of Ammon, and from the Philistines? 12 The Zidonians also, and the Amalekites, and the Maonites, did oppress you; and ye cried to me, and I delivered you out of their hand. 13 Yet ye have forsaken me, and served other gods: wherefore I will deliver you no more. 14 Go and cry unto the gods which ye have chosen; let them deliver you in the time of your tribulation. 15 And the children of Israel said unto the Lord, We have sinned: do thou unto us whatsoever seemeth good unto thee; deliver us only, we pray thee, this day. 16 And they put away the strange gods from among them, and served the Lord: and his soul was grieved for the misery of Israel. 17 Then the children of Ammon were gathered together, and encamped in Gilead. And the children of Israel assembled themselves together, and encamped in Mizpeh. 18 And the people and princes of Gilead said one to another, What man is he that will begin to

fight against the children of Ammon? he shall be head over all the inhabitants of Gilead.

10.6-18 There is ample evidence here of the lasting influence of the former inhabitants of the land, the Ammonites. The weakness of Israel again takes them down the path of Idolatry. God also allows the Philistines to literally break Israel in pieces. What a sad epitaph that it takes this to bring Israel back to her God. The predators strike defenseless Israel. God is finally ready to give up. He states He will deliver them no more (13). Go serve the Gods you have chosen. Israel recants and again puts away the gods from among them. This period, the third overall stage of the judges, extends from Jair to the rise of Samuel. This is a period of great humiliation for the nation. God gave them into the hands of not one, but two hostile nations. The Ammonites invade from the east and the Philistines from the west. The coming Judges face this crisis. Jephthah will war the Ammonites and Samson will war the Philistines. The unfinished business will eventually be left for Samuel to mop up. Seven nations had been defeated, seven foreign Gods deposed. God had delivered His people seven times, and His delivering grace was waning.

Chapter 11

11.1-3 Now Jephthah the Gileadite was a mighty man of valour, and he was the son of an harlot: and Gilead begat Jephthah. 2 And Gilead's wife bare him sons; and his wife's sons grew up, and they thrust out Jephthah, and said unto him, Thou shalt not inherit in our father's house; for thou art the son of a strange woman. 3 Then Jephthah fled from his brethren, and dwelt in the land of Tob: and there were gathered vain men to Jephthah, and went out with him.

11.1-3 Jephthah (the eastern region). Jephthah is the ninth judge of Israel and delivered God's people from 18 years of oppression by Ammon. Jephthah was an illegitimate child cast out from the family because they did not want to share the inheritance. Jephthah fled to Tob and joined himself to some worthless men. The inhabitants of Gilead summon him back to deliver them from Ammon. He is successful and makes his famous vow concerning his daughter. He later killed 42,000 of the tribe of Ephraim. He is mentioned in Hebrews 11 as a hero of faith.

11.4-10 And it came to pass in process of time, that the children of Ammon made war against Israel. 5 And it was so, that when the children of Ammon made war

against Israel, the elders of Gilead went to fetch Jephthah out of the land of Tob: 6 And they said unto Jephthah, Come, and be our captain, that we may fight with the children of Ammon. 7 And Jephthah said unto the elders of Gilead, Did not ye hate me, and expel me out of my father's house? and why are ye come unto me now when ye are in distress? 8 And the elders of Gilead said unto Jephthah, Therefore we turn again to thee now, that thou mayest go with us, and fight against the children of Ammon, and be our head over all the inhabitants of Gilead. 9 And Jephthah said unto the elders of Gilead, If ye bring me home again to fight against the children of Ammon, and the Lord deliver them before me, shall I be your head? 10 And the elders of Gilead said unto Jephthah, The Lord be witness between us, if we do not so according to thy words.

11.4-10 Gilead. This region is very luxuriant and well watered. The contrast the western part of the country is stark. Ammon claims Israel took this region from them after the exodus from Egypt, which Jephthah ignores. The story of this man draws an early parallel to Jesus. Jesus was also rejected by his brethren, then becomes the captain of our salvation. As with Jesus, Jephthah did not allow his parents to deter his mission. Jephthah realizes they turn to him in desperation, not because of love or respect.

11.11-24 Then Jephthah went with the elders of Gilead, and the people made him head and captain over them: and Jephthah uttered all his words before the Lord in Mizpeh. 12 And Jephthah sent messengers unto the king of the children of Ammon, saying, What hast thou to do with me, that thou art come against me to fight in my land? 13 And the king of the children of Ammon answered unto the messengers of Jephthah, Because

Israel took away my land, when they came up out of Egypt, from Arnon even unto Jabbok, and unto Jordan: now therefore restore those lands again peaceably. 14 And Jephthah sent messengers again unto the king of the children of Ammon: 15 And said unto him, Thus saith Jephthah, Israel took not away the land of Moab, nor the land of the children of Ammon: 16 But when Israel came up from Egypt, and walked through the wilderness unto the Red sea, and came to Kadesh; 17 Then Israel sent messengers unto the king of Edom, saying, Let me, I pray thee, pass through thy land: but the king of Edom would not hearken thereto. And in like manner they sent unto the king of Moab: but he would not consent: and Israel abode in Kadesh. 18 Then they went along through the wilderness, and compassed the land of Edom, and the land of Moab, and came by the east side of the land of Moab, and pitched on the other side of Arnon, but came not within the border of Moab: for Arnon was the border of Moab. 19 And Israel sent messengers unto Sihon king of the Amorites, the king of Heshbon; and Israel said unto him, Let us pass, we pray thee, through thy land into my place. 20 But Sihon trusted not Israel to pass through his coast: but Sihon gathered all his people together, and pitched in Jahaz, and fought against Israel. 21 And the Lord God of Israel delivered Sihon and all his people into the hand of Israel, and they smote them: so Israel possessed all the land of the Amorites, the inhabitants of that country. 22 And they possessed all the coasts of the Amorites, from Arnon even unto Jabbok, and from the wilderness even unto Jordan. 23 So now the Lord God of Israel hath dispossessed the Amorites from before his people Israel, and shouldest thou possess it? 24 Wilt not thou possess that which Chemosh thy god giveth thee to possess? So whomsoever the Lord our God shall drive out from before us, them will we possess.

11.11-24 Once Jephthah is made captain he dialogs with Ammon. The discussion rehashes old accusations. Included in the argument, Jephthah challenges them to allow their God to prove himself. This may be the catalyst that causes the writer of Hebrews to include Jephthah in the heroes of faith. Jephthah tried to negotiate without war, but was unsuccessful. Jephthah's final answer was we will see whose God is more powerful.

11.25-28 And now art thou any thing better than Balak the son of Zippor, king of Moab? did he ever strive against Israel, or did he ever fight against them, 26 While Israel dwelt in Heshbon and her towns, and in Aroer and her towns, and in all the cities that be along by the coasts of Arnon, three hundred years? why therefore did ye not recover them within that time? 27 Wherefore I have not sinned against thee, but thou doest me wrong to war against me: the Lord the Judge be judge this day between the children of Israel and the children of Ammon. 28 Howbeit the king of the children of Ammon hearkened not unto the words of Jephthah which he sent him.

11.25-28 Jephthah bolsters his argument by submitting the witness of Balak, and by extension Balaam. The King of Ammon is unconvinced so they go to war.

11.29-40 Then the Spirit of the Lord came upon Jephthah, and he passed over Gilead, and Manasseh, and passed over Mizpeh of Gilead, and from Mizpeh of Gilead he passed over unto the children of Ammon. 30 And Jephthah vowed a vow unto the Lord, and said, If thou shalt without fail deliver the children of Ammon into mine hands, 31 Then it shall be, that whatsoever cometh forth of the doors of my house to meet me, when I return in peace from the children of Ammon, shall surely be

the Lord's, and I will offer it up for a burnt offering. 32 So Jephthah passed over unto the children of Ammon to fight against them; and the Lord delivered them into his hands. 33 And he smote them from Aroer, even till thou come to Minnith, even twenty cities, and unto the plain of the vineyards, with a very great slaughter. Thus the children of Ammon were subdued before the children of Israel. 34 And Jephthah came to Mizpeh unto his house, and, behold, his daughter came out to meet him with timbrels and with dances: and she was his only child; beside her he had neither son nor daughter. 35 And it came to pass, when he saw her, that he rent his clothes, and said, Alas, my daughter! thou hast brought me very low, and thou art one of them that trouble me: for I have opened my mouth unto the Lord, and I cannot go back. 36 And she said unto him, My father, if thou hast opened thy mouth unto the Lord, do to me according to that which hath proceeded out of thy mouth; forasmuch as the Lord hath taken vengeance for thee of thine enemies, even of the children of Ammon. 37 And she said unto her father, Let this thing be done for me: let me alone two months, that I may go up and down upon the mountains, and bewail my virginity, I and my fellows. 38 And he said, Go. And he sent her away for two months: and she went with her companions, and bewailed her virginity upon the mountains. 39 And it came to pass at the end of two months, that she returned unto her father, who did with her according to his vow which he had vowed: and she knew no man. And it was a custom in Israel, 40 That the daughters of Israel went yearly to lament the daughter of Jephthah the Gileadite four days in a year.

11.29-40 The vow. Few subjects in holy scripture have been scrutinized as much as this. The answer is still inconclusive. The evidence is difficult because he says whatever comes out of his house. This limits the vow greatly. Some believe he offered his daughter as a burnt offering in the custom of the nations around him at that time (Mic 6.6-8). They argue God did not condone this, but he did not intervene. Later the prophets would rebuke this practice. It was based on giving to God your most prized possession and mirrored Abraham and Isaac. Added to this is her surrender to the vow, this is mirrored in Mary (Luke 1.38). This deep love for God would overshadow any human love by both Jephthah and his daughter. This would be cause for him to be included in the great chapter of faith in Hebrews 11. It is easy to lose sight of the world at that time because we see it 3,500 years later. Should it be the case that he offered her on a burnt offering, is this less to be pitied than the parent who lays their child on the altar of worldliness? Many parents lay their children on altars of sin, ungodliness, and unrighteousness. Do we grieve as acutely for these children as we do for this damsel offered in deep love and consecration to God? The tribute to this girl by the daughters of Israel lends further support to the finality of Jephthah's actions. She was praised each year for 4 days by the young maidens. Jephthah won the greatest of victories and paid the highest of prices. Such is life, great victory always comes at the highest price.

Chapter 12

12.1-7 And the men of Ephraim gathered themselves together, and went northward, and said unto Jephthah, Wherefore passedst thou over to fight against the children of Ammon, and didst not call us to go with thee? we will burn thine house upon thee with fire. 2 And Jephthah said unto them, I and my people were at great strife with the children of Ammon; and when I called you, ye delivered me not out of their hands. 3 And when I saw that ye delivered me not, I put my life in my hands, and passed over against the children of Ammon, and the Lord delivered them into my hand: wherefore then are ye come up unto me this day, to fight against me? 4 Then Jephthah gathered together all the men of Gilead, and fought with Ephraim: and the men of Gilead smote Ephraim, because they said, Ye Gileadites are fugitives of Ephraim among the Ephraimites, and among the Manassites. 5 And the Gileadites took the passages of Jordan before the Ephraimites: and it was so, that when those Ephraimites which were escaped said, Let me go over; that the men of Gilead said unto him, Art thou an Ephraimite? If he said, Nay; 6 Then said they unto him, Say now Shibboleth: and he said Sibboleth: for he could not frame to pronounce it right. Then they took him, and slew him at the passages of

Jordan: and there fell at that time of the Ephraimites forty and two thousand. 7 And Jephthah judged Israel six years. Then died Jephthah the Gileadite, and was buried in one of the cities of Gilead.

12.1-7 Jephthah and Ephraim. As is so often, the question arises, why? Why is this interlude placed in the scriptures? We know all scripture is given by inspiration and is profitable. What is the lesson here for the next 35 centuries? First there is the attitude of Ephraim that surfaces more than once in their history. They seemed to be easily offended and always seeking issue if they were not promoted. This proclivity is not indigent to Ephraim. It is common among many people. It is born of a deep insecurity. It fosters jealousy and strife. In this case, it ultimately cost Ephraim 42,000 men. Jephthah tried to appease with words as he had with the King of Ammon. These same Ephraimites had also fussed with Gideon in the same manner. Ephraim wanted preeminence without sacrifice. This is the second lesson from this interlude. If you want the glory then do not sit and wait for the battle to come to you. Leadership is won, not inherited.

12.8-15 And after him Ibzan of Bethlehem judged Israel. 9 And he had thirty sons, and thirty daughters, whom he sent abroad, and took in thirty daughters from abroad for his sons. And he judged Israel seven years. 10 Then died Ibzan, and was buried at Bethlehem. 11 And after him Elon, a Zebulonite, judged Israel; and he judged Israel ten years. 12 And Elon the Zebulonite died, and was buried in Aijalon in the country of Zebulun. 13 And after him Abdon the son of Hillel, a Pirathonite, judged Israel. 14 And he had forty sons and thirty nephews, that rode on threescore and ten ass colts: and he judged Israel eight years. 15 And Abdon the son of Hillel the

Pirathonite died, and was buried in Pirathon in the land of Ephraim, in the mount of the Amalekites.

12.8-15 Ibizan, Elon, and Abdon. These judges are similar to Tola and Jair. There are no deeds mentioned. It appears from the arrangement of the text, these were the successors of Jephthah. This would mean their leadership was in the east as was Jephthah's. These judges ruled for about 25 years. There appears to be no notable events in this period of time, or none that the Holy Spirit feels provides a life lesson for the following generations.

Chapter 13

13.1 And the children of Israel did evil again in the sight of the Lord; and the Lord delivered them into the hand of the Philistines forty years.

13.1 Samson. Few characters in or out of the Holy Scriptures are as polarizing as Samson. From the amazing events surrounding his birth, to his Nazarite vow, to his ill-fated marriage, to his incredible superhuman feats, and finally to his death, he captures our imagination. We are as fascinated with him as the Philistines were. His deeds of incredible strength and his bouts of weakness mesmerize us. There is no one like him anywhere in the Bible. The secular world has heard of him and is one of the very few universal known personalities outside the Bible. His larger than life persona also carries those associated with him along with him. Who would have ever heard of Delilah? She would be just another unknown loose floozy except she met Samson. At the end Samson does not die quietly in old age as many famous people of the Bible. His death is like his life, explosive to the very last moment. Yet, he is enshrined in the hall of faith of Hebrews chapter 11. Samson is a quirk of great spiritual moments and the lowest lows a man can go. No life in the Bible better portrays the nation of Israel more aptly. Samson reflects his times. Incredible victories then paralyzing failures. He is the last judge presented. Possibly this is because he is the summation of this era more than any other individual. He was a product of this time when every man did that which was right in his own eyes. His life is laid bare for us to see the result of this 450 year period where God showed man that man cannot rule himself. The greatest revelation of life is we all have a little of Samson in us.

13.2 And there was a certain man of Zorah, of the family of the Danites, whose name was Manoah; and his wife was barren, and bare not.

13.2 (the western region). This section deals with the last region mentioned. The north, central, and east areas have all been documented and now we learn of the western region. The judge raised up for this is Samson. As with the other regions, the judge himself is detailed in their life qualities. This information is about the region as well as the person. The gentle faith and overall spiritual tone of the north is embodied in Deborah. The timid, fearful faith of the central is reflected in Gideon. The reckless brash faith of the east is seen clearly in Jephthah and his vow. And now the insipid faith of the west will be made clear by this unique judge.

13.3-5 And the angel of the Lord appeared unto the woman, and said unto her, Behold now, thou art barren, and bearest not: but thou shalt conceive, and bear a son. 4 Now therefore beware, I pray thee, and drink not wine nor strong drink, and eat not any unclean thing: 5 For, lo, thou shalt conceive, and bear a son; and no razor shall come on his head: for the child shall be a Nazarite unto God from the womb: and he shall begin to deliver Israel out of the hand of the Philistines.

13.3-5 The parents of Samson. This woman is barren. Just like the western region is barren. She needs a divine miracle as does this region. A special vow is needed to jump start this area of banal faith. So God provides. Samson is an announced son. The answer to her barrenness is to live a dedicated separated life and to guide her child in the same direction. This is also what this region needed. This region had succumbed to the deities of the Philistines. This region needed inner consecration and it needed to pass that on to the next generation.

13.6-11 Then the woman came and told her husband, saying, A man of God came unto me, and his countenance was like the countenance of an angel of God, very terrible: but I asked him not whence he was, neither told he me his name:7 But he said unto me, Behold, thou shalt conceive, and bear a son; and now drink no wine nor strong drink, neither eat any unclean thing: for the child shall be a Nazarite to God from the womb to the day of his death. 8 Then Manoah intreated the Lord, and said, O my Lord, let the man of God which thou didst send come again unto us, and teach us what we shall do unto the child that shall be born. 9 And God hearkened to the voice of Manoah; and the angel of God came again unto the woman as she sat in the field: but Manoah her husband was not with her. 10 And the woman made haste, and ran, and shewed her husband, and said unto him, Behold, the man hath appeared unto me, that came unto me the other day. 11 And Manoah arose, and went after his wife, and came to the man, and said unto him, Art thou the man that spakest unto the woman? And he said, I am.

13.6-11 Manoah. This is an example that there were people all around that had held on to their faith. Another example was Boaz. Manoah seems to be a Godly man who is ready to follow a spiritual leader, even his own son. These two people present the value of godly parents and how their children can affect nations for God.

13.12-20 And Manoah said, Now let thy words come to pass. How shall we order the child, and how shall we do unto him? 13 And the angel of the Lord said unto Manoah, Of all that I said unto the woman let her beware. 14 She may not eat of any thing that cometh of the vine, neither let her drink wine or strong drink, nor eat any unclean thing: all that I commanded her let her observe. 15 And Manoah said unto the angel of the Lord, I pray thee, let us detain thee, until we shall have made ready a kid for thee. 16 And the angel of the Lord said unto Manoah, Though thou detain me, I will not eat of thy bread: and if thou wilt offer a burnt offering, thou must offer it unto the Lord. For Manoah knew not that he was an angel of the Lord. 17 And Manoah said unto the angel of the Lord, What is thy name, that when thy sayings come to pass we may do thee honour? 18 And the angel of the Lord said unto him, Why askest thou thus after my name, seeing it is secret? 19 So Manoah took a kid with a meat offering, and offered it upon a rock unto the Lord: and the angel did wonderously; and Manoah and his wife looked on. 20 For it came to pass, when the flame went up toward heaven from off the altar, that the angel of the Lord ascended in the flame of the altar. And Manoah and his wife looked on it, and fell on their faces to the ground.

13.12-20 The angel. This sequence of events is captivating. Manoah having conversation with an angel, and not knowing it was an angel. The angel patiently waiting for them. The refused food, then the ascension in the flame.

This would nail down any future doubts about Samson when his life became erratic. God was giving this couple the absolute assurance Samson was a called deliverer for all the coming moments when his actions might cause them to wonder.

13.21-25 But the angel of the Lord did no more appear to Manoah and to his wife. Then Manoah knew that he was an angel of the Lord. 22 And Manoah said unto his wife, We shall surely die, because we have seen God. 23 But his wife said unto him, If the Lord were pleased to kill us, he would not have received a burnt offering and a meat offering at our hands, neither would he have shewed us all these things, nor would as at this time have told us such things as these. 24 And the woman bare a son, and called his name Samson: and the child grew, and the Lord blessed him. 25 And the Spirit of the Lord began to move him at times in the camp of Dan between Zorah and Eshtaol.

13.21-25 Samson grows. The economy of words in the Bible frustrates us at times. We would love to be privy to some of the things Samson was doing in those early years when the spirit of the Lord moved upon him. We are left to wonder at the marvel of the moment when his parents first saw this phenomenon. The exchanged glances between them, the arched eyebrows. They at times must have stood slack jawed at what they saw. It is very possible this is why they did not object more strenuously when he asked for a Philistine bride. We are reminded, the angel of the Lord did no more appear to them. Every life reaction on their part had to be based on that initial angelic visit. We are left to wonder how many times did they wish for one more visit.

Chapter 14

14.1-10 And Samson went down to Timnath, and saw a woman in Timnath of the daughters of the Philistines. 2 And he came up, and told his father and his mother, and said, I have seen a woman in Timnath of the daughters of the Philistines: now therefore get her for me to wife. 3 Then his father and his mother said unto him, Is there never a woman among the daughters of thy brethren, or among all my people, that thou goest to take a wife of the uncircumcised Philistines? And Samson said unto his father, Get her for me; for she pleaseth me well. 4 But his father and his mother knew not that it was of the Lord, that he sought an occasion against the Philistines: for at that time the Philistines had dominion over Israel. 5 Then went Samson down, and his father and his mother, to Timnath, and came to the vineyards of Timnath: and, behold, a young lion roared against him. 6 And the Spirit of the Lord came mightily upon him, and he rent him as he would have rent a kid, and he had nothing in his hand: but he told not his father or his mother what he had done. 7 And he went down, and talked with the woman; and she pleased Samson well. 8 And after a time he returned to take her, and he turned aside to see the carcase of the lion: and, behold, there was a swarm of bees and honey in the carcase of the lion. 9 And he took thereof in his hands, and went on eating, and came to his father and mother, and he gave them, and they did eat: but he told not them that he had taken the honey out of the carcase of the lion. 10 So his father went down unto the woman: and Samson made there a feast; for so used the young men to do.

14.1-10 Samson's bride. The ways of God sometimes befuddle us. The achieving of His purpose, and the means in which he does it, at times baffles us. One thing is for sure, God does nothing by reaction. He knows where every situation is headed. Howbeit, there are times he uses people's choices to achieve an end he desires. Samson's life is a lesson in how self will is a tragic way of life. God does not allow Samson's defects and failures to abort His divine purpose. Timnath lay just across the frontier border, and the moment of Samson's marriage is a lesson in not marrying someone who is a Philistine. This marriage was trouble from the start. An unholy marriage pulls you down to levels you would not go otherwise. This is illustrated in Samson violating two of his three Nazarite vows. He touched a dead animal and attended a drinking feast. The New Testament is clear in teaching marriage should only be in the Lord.

14.11-20 And it came to pass, when they saw him, that they brought thirty companions to be with him. 12 And Samson said unto them, I will now put forth a riddle unto you: if ye can certainly declare it me within the seven days of the feast, and find it out, then I will give you thirty sheets and thirty change of garments: 13 But if ye cannot declare it me, then shall ye give me thirty sheets and thirty change of garments. And they said unto him, Put forth thy riddle, that we may hear it. 14 And he

said unto them, Out of the eater came forth meat, and out of the strong came forth sweetness. And they could not in three days expound the riddle. 15 And it came to pass on the seventh day, that they said unto Samson's wife, Entice thy husband, that he may declare unto us the riddle, lest we burn thee and thy father's house with fire: have ye called us to take that we have? is it not so? 16 And Samson's wife wept before him, and said, Thou dost but hate me, and lovest me not: thou hast put forth a riddle unto the children of my people, and hast not told it me. And he said unto her, Behold, I have not told it my father nor my mother, and shall I tell it thee? 17 And she wept before him the seven days, while their feast lasted: and it came to pass on the seventh day, that he told her, because she lay sore upon him: and she told the riddle to the children of her people. 18 And the men of the city said unto him on the seventh day before the sun went down, What is sweeter than honey? And what is stronger than a lion? and he said unto them, If ye had not plowed with my heifer, ye had not found out my riddle. 19 And the Spirit of the Lord came upon him, and he went down to Ashkelon, and slew thirty men of them, and took their spoil, and gave change of garments unto them which expounded the riddle. And his anger was kindled, and he went up to his father's house. 20 But Samson's wife was given to his companion, whom he had used as his friend.

14.11-20 The riddle. The riddles of life are always born of our failures. The whys of our life never center on when we obeyed. It is the dark moments and our weak moments that cause us riddles. This riddle was drawn from Samson breaking his vow. His vow hid the riddle from the 30 men who were trying to figure it out. He did not touch dead things, so they never mentally went there. This principal is the fountain of guilt and shame on all men. The secret failures that no one observes provide the riddles of life we cannot solve.

Chapter 15

15.1-5 But it came to pass within a while after, in the time of wheat harvest, that Samson visited his wife with a kid; and he said, I will go in to my wife into the chamber. But her father would not suffer him to go in. 2 And her father said, I verily thought that thou hadst utterly hated her; therefore I gave her to thy companion: is not her younger sister fairer than she? take her, I pray thee, instead of her. 3 And Samson said concerning them, Now shall I be more blameless than the Philistines, though I do them a displeasure. 4 And Samson went and caught three hundred foxes, and took firebrands, and turned tail to tail, and put a firebrand in the midst between two tails. 5 And when he had set the brands on fire, he let them go into the standing corn of the Philistines, and burnt up both the shocks, and also the standing corn, with the vineyards and olives.

15.1-5 The foxes. Time had passed and the anger of Samson had waned. To reconcile with his wife he takes a gift and goes to see her. This altercation is to be the launchpad of one of his most heroic feats. His father in law has given his wife to another so Samson seeks revenge. Whether he caught jackals (which run in groups) or foxes (which are solitary), it is an amazing feat. These animals are numerous in Palestine and are mentioned several places in the scriptures. Probably at nightfall Samson sends these animals with fire tied to their tails into the Shefala of Philistia. The Shefala is the plain of Philistia where their corn was grown and was on the border of Dan and Judah. This was a fertile plain where much corn was grown. The fire spread to the vineyards and olive groves. The Philistines were getting some of the same medicine they had doled out to Israel. It is apropos that Samson's wife revealed the riddle to avoid being burned with fire, and she ultimately ends up suffering that exact judgment at the hands of her countrymen. So often the thing we give up to appease unrighteousness, comes back to be our defeat.

15.6-20 Then the Philistines said, Who hath done this? And they answered, Samson, the son in law of the Timnite, because he had taken his wife, and given her to his companion. And the Philistines came up, and burnt her and her father with fire. 7 And Samson said unto them, Though ye have done this, yet will I be avenged of you, and after that I will cease. 8 And he smote them hip and thigh with a great slaughter: and he went down and dwelt in the top of the rock Etam. 9 Then the Philistines went up, and pitched in Judah, and spread themselves in Lehi. 10 And the men of Judah said, Why are ye come up against us? And they answered, To bind Samson are we come up, to do to him as he hath done to us. 11 Then three thousand men of Judah went to the top of the rock Etam, and said to Samson, Knowest thou not that the Philistines are rulers over us? what is this that thou hast done unto us? And he said unto them, As they did unto me, so have I done unto them. 12 And they said unto him, We are come down to bind thee, that we may deliver thee into the hand of the Philistines. And Samson said unto them, Swear unto me, that ye will not

fall upon me yourselves. 13 And they spake unto him, saying, No; but we will bind thee fast, and deliver thee into their hand: but surely we will not kill thee. And they bound him with two new cords, and brought him up from the rock. 14 And when he came unto Lehi, the Philistines shouted against him: and the Spirit of the Lord came mightily upon him, and the cords that were upon his arms became as flax that was burnt with fire, and his bands loosed from off his hands. 15 And he found a new jawbone of an ass, and put forth his hand, and took it, and slew a thousand men therewith. 16 And Samson said, With the jawbone of an ass, heaps upon heaps, with the jaw of an ass have I slain a thousand men. 17 And it came to pass, when he had made an end of speaking, that he cast away the jawbone out of his hand, and called that place Ramathlehi. 18 And he was sore athirst, and called on the Lord, and said, Thou hast given this great deliverance into the hand of thy servant: and now shall I die for thirst, and fall into the hand of the uncircumcised? 19 But God clave an hollow place that was in the jaw, and there came water thereout; and when he had drunk, his spirit came again, and he revived: wherefore he called the name thereof Enhakkore, which is in Lehi unto this day. 20 And he judged Israel in the days of the Philistines twenty years.

15.6-20 This event gave birth to an even greater heroic event. The angry Philistines seek to kill Samson and he has a running battle with them and defeats them. Samson is unique as a judge in that he is never a general or leads an army. The other judges mostly led armies. He could not lead men any more than he could control his own desires. Samson flees to a fortified place called the rock of Etam. It is here in the place of the falcon or hawk (etam) that Samson's most famous victory occurs. Judah sends

3,000 men to seek the cause of the problem and they leave Samson to fight alone. Judah sells him out to save themselves. Judah binds him and delivers Samson to the Philistines. It is of note that Samson was not recognized by his own brethren as a deliverer. The refrain of Samson in verse 16 concerning heap upon heaps indicates a running battle of sorts. It appears the Philistines began to flee and Samson pursued and left more than one heap of dead enemies. It has been debated if it was a literal 1000 men or if this number represents a great multitude. The word is used over 500 times and almost universally means a literal number. The law of Hermeneutics would dictate if it can be literal, it is literal. This jawbone today would be enshrined in a museum somewhere, but Samson casts it away. The power was not in the bone but rather in the benevolence of the Lord. He names the place Enhakhore the fountain of one calling. He is still listed as judging Israel 20 years and is listed in Hebrews 11 as a hero of faith, even though he was a lone wolf judge.

Chapter 16

16.1-3 Then went Samson to Gaza, and saw there an harlot, and went in unto her. 2 And it was told the Gazites, saying, Samson is come hither. And they compassed him in, and laid wait for him all night in the gate of the city, and were quiet all the night, saying, In the morning, when it is day, we shall kill him. 3 And Samson lay till midnight, and arose at midnight, and took the doors of the gate of the city, and the two posts, and went away with them, bar and all, and put them upon his shoulders, and carried them up to the top of an hill that is before Hebron.

16.1-3 The harlot and the gates of Gaza. This is one of the moments of Samson's life that perplexes us. We see his low moments and then quickly he turns and achieves an inhuman feat. He stays with the harlot until midnight, then rips the gates of the city, which weigh an incredible weight right off the wall, and carries them 38 miles uphill to Hebron. Our minds struggle with this. How? Why? How can he go from such wrong to such right so quickly? The harlot is the second woman involving Samson, the third will be Delilah. We are left to wonder what the outcome might have been had Samson been connected to a godly woman like Deborah. Is the midnight hour significant here? Many momentous events happen at midnight in the Bible. Why did he awaken? Why did he rip the gates off? Why carry them so far away? All these bizarre connections cause us to wonder. One suggestion is the foreshadowing of the coming of Jesus Christ who would assail the very gates of hell and free the captives from Abraham's bosom. Ps 24.7 "Lift up your heads, O ye gates; and be ye lift up, ye everlasting doors; and the King of glory shall come in." Who is this King of glory? The Lord of hosts, he is the King of glory.

16.4-22 And it came to pass afterward, that he loved a woman in the valley of Sorek, whose name was Delilah. 5 And the lords of the Philistines came up unto her, and said unto her, Entice him, and see wherein his great strength lieth, and by what means we may prevail against him, that we may bind him to afflict him; and we will give thee every one of us eleven hundred pieces of silver. 6 And Delilah said to Samson, Tell me, I pray thee, wherein thy great strength lieth, and wherewith thou mightest be bound to afflict thee. 7 And Samson said unto her, If they bind me with seven green withs that were never dried, then shall I be weak, and be as another man. 8 Then the lords of the Philistines brought up to her seven green withs which had not been dried, and she bound him with them. 9 Now there were men lying in wait, abiding with her in the chamber. And she said unto him, The Philistines be upon thee, Samson. And he brake the withs, as a thread of tow is broken when it toucheth the fire. So his strength was not known. 10 And Delilah said unto Samson, Behold, thou hast mocked me, and told me lies: now tell me, I pray thee, wherewith thou mightest be bound. 11 And he said unto her, If they bind me fast with new ropes that never were occupied, then shall I be weak, and be as another man.

12 Delilah therefore took new ropes, and bound him therewith, and said unto him, The Philistines be upon thee, Samson. And there were liers in wait abiding in the chamber. And he brake them from off his arms like a thread. 13 And Delilah said unto Samson, Hitherto thou hast mocked me, and told me lies: tell me wherewith thou mightest be bound. And he said unto her, If thou weavest the seven locks of my head with the web. 14 And she fastened it with the pin, and said unto him, The Philistines be upon thee, Samson. And he awaked out of his sleep, and went away with the pin of the beam, and with the web. 15 And she said unto him, How canst thou say, I love thee, when thine heart is not with me? thou hast mocked me these three times, and hast not told me wherein thy great strength lieth. 16 And it came to pass, when she pressed him daily with her words, and urged him, so that his soul was vexed unto death; 17 That he told her all his heart, and said unto her, There hath not come a razor upon mine head; for I have been a Nazarite unto God from my mother's womb: if I be shaven, then my strength will go from me, and I shall become weak, and be like any other man. 18 And when Delilah saw that he had told her all his heart, she sent and called for the lords of the Philistines, saying, Come up this once, for he hath shewed me all his heart. Then the lords of the Philistines came up unto her, and brought money in their hand. 19 And she made him sleep upon her knees; and she called for a man, and she caused him to shave off the seven locks of his head; and she began to afflict him, and his strength went from him. 20 And she said, The Philistines be upon thee, Samson. And he awoke out of his sleep, and said, I will go out as at other times before, and shake myself. And he wist not that the Lord was departed from him. 21 But the Philistines took him, and put out his eyes, and brought him down to Gaza,

and bound him with fetters of brass; and he did grind in the prison house. 22 Howbeit the hair of his head began to grow again after he was shaven.

16.4-22 Delilah. History has offered us a few women who are infamous worldwide. Delilah joins the likes of Jezebel and Cleopatra for universal recognition. Her name is synonymous with treachery. We again muse what Samson saw in her. All three women he was connected with were Philistines, and all three showed no love for him. To Delilah, Samson was a cash cow who would fatten her purse by 5,500 pieces of silver. Delilah was a gold digger. It is a mystery to us that Samson could not ever see through his relationships and see the deceit. Was God trying to illustrate to Israel how they were treating Him? Israel, God's chosen wife, was not promising to be much better than Samson's choices. Israel was selling God out for grain. Israel also turned to the five lords of the Philistines for rewards, and sold their deliverer out as well by turning to idols. The life portrait here is being painted on a living canvas for Israel to see. Before we indict Delilah, we should always inventory our own heart to insure we are not guilty of the same actions.

16.23-31 Then the lords of the Philistines gathered them together for to offer a great sacrifice unto Dagon their god, and to rejoice: for they said, Our god hath delivered Samson our enemy into our hand. 24 And when the people saw him, they praised their god: for they said, Our god hath delivered into our hands our enemy, and the destroyer of our country, which slew many of us. 25 And it came to pass, when their hearts were merry, that they said, Call for Samson, that he may make us sport. And they called for Samson out of the prison house; and he made them sport: and they set him between the pillars.

26 And Samson said unto the lad that held him by the hand, Suffer me that I may feel the pillars whereupon the house standeth, that I may lean upon them. 27 Now the house was full of men and women; and all the lords of the Philistines were there; and there were upon the roof about three thousand men and women, that beheld while Samson made sport. 28 And Samson called unto the Lord, and said, O Lord God, remember me, I pray thee, and strengthen me, I pray thee, only this once, O God, that I may be at once avenged of the Philistines for my two eyes. 29 And Samson took hold of the two middle pillars upon which the house stood, and on which it was borne up, of the one with his right hand, and of the other with his left. 30 And Samson said, Let me die with the Philistines. And he bowed himself with all his might; and the house fell upon the lords, and upon all the people that were therein. So the dead which he slew at his death were more than they which he slew in his life. 31 Then his brethren and all the house of his father came down, and took him, and brought him up, and buried him between Zorah and Eshtaol in the buryingplace of Manoah his father. And he judged Israel twenty years.

16.23-31 Samson's death. Samson was now blind. Actually, he had been spiritually blind all along. The deliverer of Israel is out of sight for a while, but when he returns it is with great victory. The victory at Samson's death is one of the great Old Testament moments. The shadow of this moment reaches all the way to the coming of our deliverer. Jesus is away for a while, but our deliverer will come again and when He does the whole house of the Philistines (the wicked) will fall. Samson, the lone wolf deliverer, brings his greatest victory at his death. Jesus Christ, our great deliverer, brought His greatest victory at His death on Calvary.

Chapter 17

17.1 And there was a man of mount Ephraim, whose name was Micah.

17.1 The book of Judges is unique in this section of the remaining chapters. These five chapters are an appendix, a summation, and an overview of the times. They reveal the core of the people in this era, and reveal its subsequent consequences. Things start here that take a thousand years to eradicate. The events in this book are difficult to place on a timeline. Some postulate they are in sequence. Another view places them in geographical settings, beginning in the north with Deborah, moving to the center with Gideon, then the east with Jephthah, and finally the west with Samson. None of the judges ruled over the entire 12 tribes, all of them were regional at best. The major theme is there was no king in those days and every man did that which was right in his own eyes. Ultimately this was disastrous. In the mix of failure and idolatry there were those who never compromised. Boaz in the book of Ruth, is an example of a faithful man in the midst of wholesale departure from truth. Spiritual compromise always leads to moral corruption.

17.2-13 And he said unto his mother, The eleven

hundred shekels of silver that were taken from thee, about which thou cursedst, and spakest of also in mine ears, behold, the silver is with me; I took it. And his mother said, Blessed be thou of the Lord, my son. 3 And when he had restored the eleven hundred shekels of silver to his mother, his mother said, I had wholly dedicated the silver unto the Lord from my hand for my son, to make a graven image and a molten image: now therefore I will restore it unto thee. 4 Yet he restored the money unto his mother; and his mother took two hundred shekels of silver, and gave them to the founder, who made thereof a graven image and a molten image: and they were in the house of Micah. 5 And the man Micah had an house of gods, and made an ephod, and teraphim, and consecrated one of his sons, who became his priest. 6 In those days there was no king in Israel, but every man did that which was right in his own eyes. 7 And there was a young man out of Bethlehemjudah of the family of Judah, who was a Levite, and he sojourned there. 8 And the man departed out of the city from Bethlehemjudah to sojourn where he could find a place: and he came to mount Ephraim to the house of Micah, as he journeyed. 9 And Micah said unto him, Whence comest thou? And he said unto him, I am a Levite of Bethlehemjudah, and I go to sojourn where I may find a place. 10 And Micah said unto him, Dwell with me, and be unto me a father and a priest, and I will give thee ten shekels of silver by the year, and a suit of apparel, and thy victuals. So the Levite went in. 11 And the Levite was content to dwell with the man; and the young man was unto him as one of his sons. 12 And Micah consecrated the Levite; and the young man became his priest, and was in the house of Micah. 13 Then said Micah, Now know I that the Lord will do me good, seeing I have a Levite to my priest.

17.2-13 The genesis of idolatry. This introduces us to the DNA of idolatry. How did a people with such a magnificent beginning end up being entangled with idols for a thousand years? The introduction of image worship, and the final story of Israel warring against each other, are the two major points in these last five chapters. Woven into these are the tribe of Dan moving from its inheritance in the south to the north. Micah attempts to put a religious spin on his idolatrous image by inviting a Levite to be his priest. This proves to ultimately be the most damning part of Israel's idolatry. Israel tried to blend her religion with other religions. This is always more reprehensible in the eyes of God. The wandering Levite gets hired as a personal priest to Micah. This is a complete reversal in every way of the purpose of the tribe of Levi. The tribe of Levi was to serve the entire nation as priests, and their inheritance of tithe and offering supported them. The spirit of God is writing for all future generations to see the result of man-made religion. The New Testament speaks of pure religion in James 1.27. It uses the term undefiled. The universal failure of man is always manifested in his attempt to improve on what God has set in place. The result? Spoiled, defiled, religion. It reeks of a single drop of poison in a fresh clear glass of water. James says this kind of religion is vain, empty and profitless. This type of religion produces what occurs in the next chapters of Judges. Mayhem, murder and molestation rule the land.

Chapter 18

18.1 In those days there was no king in Israel: and in those days the tribe of the Danites sought them an inheritance to dwell in; for unto that day all their inheritance had not fallen unto them among the tribes of Israel.

18.1 Dan. This interlude sets forth an important principal. It shows the consequences of not being satisfied with your inheritance. The tribe of Dan was not content with what had been given to them. They were in the west toward the south. They chose to abandon what God had allocated them and choose a new inheritance. The consequences of this is the removal of any legacy of Dan in the rest of the Bible. One descendant is mentioned as helping in the construction of the temple. In Revelation when the 12 tribes are listed, Dan has been eliminated. This concept was being highlighted by the anointing spirit upon the writer of Judges. The consequences of not being satisfied with your inheritance is you will be removed from the people of God.

18.2-12 And the children of Dan sent of their family five men from their coasts, men of valour, from Zorah, and from Eshtaol, to spy out the land, and to search it; and they said unto them, Go, search the land: who when they

came to mount Ephraim, to the house of Micah, they lodged there. 3 When they were by the house of Micah, they knew the voice of the young man the Levite: and they turned in thither, and said unto him, Who brought thee hither? and what makest thou in this place? and what hast thou here? 4 And he said unto them, Thus and thus dealeth Micah with me, and hath hired me, and I am his priest. 5 And they said unto him, Ask counsel, we pray thee, of God, that we may know whether our way which we go shall be prosperous. 6 And the priest said unto them, Go in peace: before the Lord is your way wherein ye go. 7 Then the five men departed, and came to Laish, and saw the people that were therein, how they dwelt careless, after the manner of the Zidonians, quiet and secure; and there was no magistrate in the land, that might put them to shame in any thing; and they were far from the Zidonians, and had no business with any man. 8 And they came unto their brethren to Zorah and Eshtaol: and their brethren said unto them, What say ye? 9 And they said, Arise, that we may go up against them: for we have seen the land, and, behold, it is very good: and are ye still? be not slothful to go, and to enter to possess the land. 10 When ye go, ye shall come unto a people secure, and to a large land: for God hath given it into your hands; a place where there is no want of any thing that is in the earth. 11 And there went from thence of the family of the Danites, out of Zorah and out of Eshtaol, six hundred men appointed with weapons of war. 12 And they went up, and pitched in Kirjathjearim, in Judah: wherefore they called that place Mahanehdan unto this day: behold, it is behind Kirjathjearim.

18.2-12 It is at the house of Micah with his hired priest that Dan gets religious approval for his journey to destruction. The approval of a priest does not always signify the approval of God. Sadly, Dan and all his future posterity are cursed by trusting a religious voice that was not ordained by God. The result was Dan was removed from any inheritance because he disdained the inheritance God allocated him.

18.13-31 And they passed thence unto mount Ephraim, and came unto the house of Micah. 14 Then answered the five men that went to spy out the country of Laish, and said unto their brethren, Do ye know that there is in these houses an ephod, and teraphim, and a graven image, and a molten image? now therefore consider what ye have to do. 15 And they turned thitherward, and came to the house of the young man the Levite, even unto the house of Micah, and saluted him. 16 And the six hundred men appointed with their weapons of war, which were of the children of Dan, stood by the entering of the gate. 17 And the five men that went to spy out the land went up, and came in thither, and took the graven image, and the ephod, and the teraphim, and the molten image: and the priest stood in the entering of the gate with the six hundred men that were appointed with weapons of war. 18 And these went into Micah's house, and fetched the carved image, the ephod, and the teraphim, and the molten image. Then said the priest unto them, What do ye? 19 And they said unto him, Hold thy peace, lay thine hand upon thy mouth, and go with us, and be to us a father and a priest: is it better for thee to be a priest unto the house of one man, or that thou be a priest unto a tribe and a family in Israel? 20 And the priest's heart was glad, and he took the ephod, and the teraphim, and the graven image, and went in the midst of the people. 21 So they turned and departed, and put the little ones and the cattle and the carriage before them. 22 And when they were a good way from the house of Micah, the men that

were in the houses near to Micah's house were gathered together, and overtook the children of Dan. 23 And they cried unto the children of Dan. And they turned their faces, and said unto Micah, What aileth thee, that thou comest with such a company? 24 And he said, Ye have taken away my gods which I made, and the priest, and ye are gone away: and what have I more? and what is this that ye say unto me, What aileth thee? 25 And the children of Dan said unto him, Let not thy voice be heard among us, lest angry fellows run upon thee, and thou lose thy life, with the lives of thy household. 26 And the children of Dan went their way: and when Micah saw that they were too strong for him, he turned and went back unto his house. 27 And they took the things which Micah had made, and the priest which he had, and came unto Laish, unto a people that were at quiet and secure: and they smote them with the edge of the sword, and burnt the city with fire. 28 And there was no deliverer, because it was far from Zidon, and they had no business with any man; and it was in the valley that lieth by Bethrehob. And they built a city, and dwelt therein. 29 And they called the name of the city Dan, after the name of Dan their father, who was born unto Israel: howbeit the name of the city was Laish at the first. 30 And the children of Dan set up the graven image: and Jonathan, the son of Gershom, the son of Manasseh, he and his sons were priests to the tribe of Dan until the day of the captivity of the land. 31 And they set them up Micah's graven image, which he made, all the time that the house of God was in Shiloh.

18.13-31 Having been given religious approval, the tribe of Dan now feels justified to proceed. As they make the move to oblivion, they stop long enough to force the hired priest to join their rebellion, for he has sanctioned it. Dan takes the gods of Micah and indentures the hired priest. The priest confiscates the gods and ephod that are not his, and joins Dan's rebellion. When Micah pleads for restoration, he is scorned. The writer of Judges is showing all future generations what the heart of man is capable of when true religion is cast aside. Once Dan has relocated, he sets up his false image and puts his hired priests in place. Rebellion has birthed idolatry. Murder and mayhem have now been given religious sanction. This is the DNA of rebellion and idolatry. Every man doing what is right in his own eyes.

Chapter 19

19.1-21 And it came to pass in those days, when there was no king in Israel, that there was a certain Levite sojourning on the side of mount Ephraim, who took to him a concubine out of Bethlehemjudah. 2 And his concubine played the whore against him, and went away from him unto her father's house to Bethlehemjudah, and was there four whole months. 3 And her husband arose, and went after her, to speak friendly unto her, and to bring her again, having his servant with him, and a couple of asses: and she brought him into her father's house: and when the father of the damsel saw him, he rejoiced to meet him. 4 And his father in law, the damsel's father, retained him; and he abode with him three days: so they did eat and drink, and lodged there. 5 And it came to pass on the fourth day, when they arose early in the morning, that he rose up to depart: and the damsel's father said unto his son in law, Comfort thine heart with a morsel of bread, and afterward go your way. 6 And they sat down, and did eat and drink both of them together: for the damsel's father had said unto the man, Be content, I pray thee, and tarry all night, and let thine heart be merry. 7 And when the man rose up to depart, his father in law urged him: therefore he lodged there again. 8 And he arose early in the morning on the fifth day to depart; and the damsel's father said, Comfort thine heart, I pray thee. And they tarried until afternoon, and they did eat both of them. 9 And when the man rose up to depart, he, and his concubine, and his servant, his father in law, the damsel's father, said unto him, Behold, now the day draweth toward evening, I pray you tarry all night: behold, the day groweth to an end, lodge here, that thine heart may be merry; and to morrow get you early on your way, that thou mayest go home. 10 But the man would not tarry that night, but he rose up and departed, and came over against Jebus, which is Jerusalem; and there were with him two asses saddled, his concubine also was with him. 11 And when they were by Jebus, the day was far spent; and the servant said unto his master, Come, I pray thee, and let us turn in into this city of the Jebusites, and lodge in it. 12 And his master said unto him, We will not turn aside hither into the city of a stranger, that is not of the children of Israel; we will pass over to Gibeah. 13 And he said unto his servant, Come, and let us draw near to one of these places to lodge all night, in Gibeah, or in Ramah. 14 And they passed on and went their way; and the sun went down upon them when they were by Gibeah, which belongeth to Benjamin. 15 And they turned aside thither, to go in and to lodge in Gibeah: and when he went in, he sat him down in a street of the city: for there was no man that took them into his house to lodging. 16 And, behold, there came an old man from his work out of the field at even, which was also of mount Ephraim; and he sojourned in Gibeah: but the men of the place were Benjamites. 17 And when he had lifted up his eyes, he saw a wayfaring man in the street of the city: and the old man said, Whither goest thou? and whence comest thou? 18 And he said unto him, We are passing from Bethlehemjudah toward the side of mount Ephraim;

from thence am I: and I went to Bethlehemjudah, but I am now going to the house of the Lord; and there is no man that receiveth me to house. 19 Yet there is both straw and provender for our asses; and there is bread and wine also for me, and for thy handmaid, and for the young man which is with thy servants: there is no want of any thing. 20 And the old man said, Peace be with thee; howsoever let all thy wants lie upon me; only lodge not in the street. 21 So he brought him into his house, and gave provender unto the asses: and they washed their feet, and did eat and drink.

19.1-21 The concubine. The subject of concubines is a difficult one for the western mind to grasp. Why was this allowed? Is it ok today? Why a concubine and not a wife? The first consideration is there were no provisions for a woman if she was without support of father, family, or husband. She had no social assistance to turn to. Secondly, due to wars and their prevalence there were usually more women in the society than men. This left women without any means of support. She was left with the option of being a harlot or prostitute, or becoming a concubine. A concubine had no wedding dowry to give her husband. God did not institute this way of life any more than He did slavery. What God did in the Old Testament was regulate the social customs of that historical era to provide fairness and equity. This was why the social institution of concubines existed in that day and not today. Today we have provisions for women and children who are destitute. A concubine in some ways was not the equal of a wife for no dowry had been provided. In other ways a concubine was equal in being supported and provided for as we see in the 12 tribes of Israel. In this chapter the concubine of a Levite is abused and therefore falls under the same consideration as a wife because protection was provided for concubines. The ensuing battle and its consequences would not be different if she had been a wife of the Levite.

19.22-30 Now as they were making their hearts merry, behold, the men of the city, certain sons of Belial, beset the house round about, and beat at the door, and spake to the master of the house, the old man, saying, Bring forth the man that came into thine house, that we may know him. 23 And the man, the master of the house, went out unto them, and said unto them, Nay, my brethren, nay, I pray you, do not so wickedly; seeing that this man is come into mine house, do not this folly. 24 Behold, here is my daughter a maiden, and his concubine; them I will bring out now, and humble ye them, and do with them what seemeth good unto you: but unto this man do not so vile a thing. 25 But the men would not hearken to him: so the man took his concubine, and brought her forth unto them; and they knew her, and abused her all the night until the morning: and when the day began to spring, they let her go. 26 Then came the woman in the dawning of the day, and fell down at the door of the man's house where her lord was, till it was light. 27 And her lord rose up in the morning, and opened the doors of the house, and went out to go his way: and, behold, the woman his concubine was fallen down at the door of the house, and her hands were upon the threshold. 28 And he said unto her, Up, and let us be going. But none answered. Then the man took her up upon an ass, and the man rose up, and gat him unto his place. 29 And when he was come into his house, he took a knife, and laid hold on his concubine, and divided her, together with her bones, into twelve pieces, and sent her into all the coasts of Israel. 30 And it was so, that all that saw it said, There was no such deed done nor seen from the day that the children of Israel came up out of the land

of Egypt unto this day: consider of it, take advice, and speak your minds.

19.22-30 This event transpires early in the book of Judges because Phinehas is the high priest (20.28), so this event occurred soon after the death of Joshua. This chapter records the crime, chapter 20 records the war that resulted, and chapter 21 is the preservation of the tribe of Benjamin from complete extinction. This is supported by the fact the entire nation goes to war and this is the only time in the entire book we know of this happening. Therefore, the sin was egregious and was offensive to every man in Israel. This crime touched a nerve so deep in every man that every tribe mobilized for war. Eventually 65,000 men will die over this issue. This totals more casualties than all the wars of the seven nations combined. The inner war of Israel between her own tribes killed more than the wars fought against the heathen nations. The enemy within is more dangerous than the enemy without.

Chapter 20

20.1-16 Then all the children of Israel went out, and the congregation was gathered together as one man, from Dan even to Beersheba, with the land of Gilead, unto the Lord in Mizpeh. 2 And the chief of all the people, even of all the tribes of Israel, presented themselves in the assembly of the people of God, four hundred thousand footmen that drew sword. 3 (Now the children of Benjamin heard that the children of Israel were gone up to Mizpeh.) Then said the children of Israel, Tell us, how was this wickedness? 4 And the Levite, the husband of the woman that was slain, answered and said, I came into Gibeah that belongeth to Benjamin, I and my concubine, to lodge. 5 And the men of Gibeah rose against me, and beset the house round about upon me by night, and thought to have slain me: and my concubine have they forced, that she is dead. 6 And I took my concubine, and cut her in pieces, and sent her throughout all the country of the inheritance of Israel: for they have committed lewdness and folly in Israel. 7 Behold, ye are all children of Israel; give here your advice and counsel. 8 And all the people arose as one man, saying, We will not any of us go to his tent, neither will we any of us turn into his house. 9 But now this shall be the thing which we will do to Gibeah; we will go up by lot against it; 10 And we will take ten men of an hundred throughout all the tribes of Israel, and an hundred of a thousand, and a thousand out of ten thousand, to fetch victual for the people, that they may do, when they come to Gibeah of Benjamin, according to all the folly that they have wrought in Israel. 11 So all the men of Israel were gathered against the city, knit together as one man. 12 And the tribes of Israel sent men through all the tribe of Benjamin, saying, What wickedness is this that is done among you? 13 Now therefore deliver us the men, the children of Belial, which are in Gibeah, that we may put them to death, and put away evil from Israel. But the children of Benjamin would not hearken to the voice of their brethren the children of Israel. 14 But the children of Benjamin gathered themselves together out of the cities unto Gibeah, to go out to battle against the children of Israel. 15 And the children of Benjamin were numbered at that time out of the cities twenty and six thousand men that drew sword, beside the inhabitants of Gibeah, which were numbered seven hundred chosen men. 16 Among all this people there were seven hundred chosen men lefthanded; every one could sling stones at an hair breadth, and not miss.

20.1-16 The evidence. This entire story is horrible beyond comprehension. There is the Levite who could have divorced the concubine under the law but chose to reconcile. There is the concubine who played the whore. Then the Levite surrenders her to the sons of Belial. These men were worthless and evil. This title of Belial is later given to Satan himself. The leaders of the tribes investigate the charge and the evidence. The decision is made this cannot go unchallenged. The tribe of Benjamin is asked to give up the offenders. Benjamin refuses for reasons we cannot fathom.

20.17-48 And the men of Israel, beside Benjamin, were numbered four hundred thousand men that drew sword: all these were men of war. 18 And the children of Israel arose, and went up to the house of God, and asked counsel of God, and said, Which of us shall go up first to the battle against the children of Benjamin? And the Lord said, Judah shall go up first. 19 And the children of Israel rose up in the morning, and encamped against Gibeah. 20 And the men of Israel went out to battle against Benjamin; and the men of Israel put themselves in array to fight against them at Gibeah. 21 And the children of Benjamin came forth out of Gibeah, and destroyed down to the ground of the Israelites that day twenty and two thousand men. 22 And the people the men of Israel encouraged themselves, and set their battle again in array in the place where they put themselves in array the first day. 23 (And the children of Israel went up and wept before the Lord until even, and asked counsel of the Lord, saying, Shall I go up again to battle against the children of Benjamin my brother? And the Lord said, Go up against him.) 24 And the children of Israel came near against the children of Benjamin the second day. 25 And Benjamin went forth against them out of Gibeah the second day, and destroyed down to the ground of the children of Israel again eighteen thousand men; all these drew the sword. 26 Then all the children of Israel, and all the people, went up, and came unto the house of God, and wept, and sat there before the Lord, and fasted that day until even, and offered burnt offerings and peace offerings before the Lord. 27 And the children of Israel enquired of the Lord, (for the ark of the covenant of God was there in those days, 28 And Phinehas, the son of Eleazar, the son of Aaron, stood before it in those days,) saying, Shall I yet again go out to battle against the children of Benjamin my brother, or shall I cease?

And the Lord said, Go up; for to morrow I will deliver them into thine hand. 29 And Israel set liers in wait round about Gibeah. 30 And the children of Israel went up against the children of Benjamin on the third day, and put themselves in array against Gibeah, as at other times. 31 And the children of Benjamin went out against the people, and were drawn away from the city; and they began to smite of the people, and kill, as at other times, in the highways, of which one goeth up to the house of God, and the other to Gibeah in the field, about thirty men of Israel. 32 And the children of Benjamin said, They are smitten down before us, as at the first. But the children of Israel said, Let us flee, and draw them from the city unto the highways. 33 And all the men of Israel rose up out of their place, and put themselves in array at Baaltamar: and the liers in wait of Israel came forth out of their places, even out of the meadows of Gibeah. 34 And there came against Gibeah ten thousand chosen men out of all Israel, and the battle was sore: but they knew not that evil was near them. 35 And the Lord smote Benjamin before Israel: and the children of Israel destroyed of the Benjamites that day twenty and five thousand and an hundred men: all these drew the sword. 36 So the children of Benjamin saw that they were smitten: for the men of Israel gave place to the Benjamites, because they trusted unto the liers in wait which they had set beside Gibeah. 37 And the liers in wait hasted, and rushed upon Gibeah; and the liers in wait drew themselves along, and smote all the city with the edge of the sword. 38 Now there was an appointed sign between the men of Israel and the liers in wait, that they should make a great flame with smoke rise up out of the city. 39 And when the men of Israel retired in the battle, Benjamin began to smite and kill of the men of Israel about thirty persons: for they said, Surely they are smitten down before us, as in the first battle. 40 But when the flame began to arise up out of the city with a pillar of smoke, the Benjamites looked behind them, and, behold, the flame of the city ascended up to heaven. 41 And when the men of Israel turned again, the men of Benjamin were amazed: for they saw that evil was come upon them. 42 Therefore they turned their backs before the men of Israel unto the way of the wilderness; but the battle overtook them; and them which came out of the cities they destroyed in the midst of them. 43 Thus they inclosed the Benjamites round about, and chased them, and trode them down with ease over against Gibeah toward the sunrising. 44 And there fell of Benjamin eighteen thousand men; all these were men of valour. 45 And they turned and fled toward the wilderness unto the rock of Rimmon: and they gleaned of them in the highways five thousand men; and pursued hard after them unto Gidom, and slew two thousand men of them. 46 So that all which fell that day of Benjamin were twenty and five thousand men that drew the sword; all these were men of valour. 47 But six hundred men turned and fled to the wilderness unto the rock Rimmon, and abode in the rock Rimmon four months. 48 And the men of Israel turned again upon the children of Benjamin, and smote them with the edge of the sword, as well the men of every city, as the beast, and all that came to hand: also they set on fire all the cities that they came to.

20.17-48 There is a very detailed account of this battle. When God places exact details in the scripture it behooves us to pay attention. We are privy to their attitude, to their plans, and to their prudence by having these details. Like an archaeological find this provides us with understanding of their time. This is easier to understand when we realize this occurred at the beginning of the time of the Judges.

This particular mobilization of the tribes was not long after they had done this numerous times to invade the land. Had this event happened at the end of the four hundred and fifty years the assembling of the tribes might not have happened. The men of Israel follow the same customs of war they used in the invasion and conquest of Palestine. They killed the inhabitants and burned the cities. Ten percent of the army of Israel fell in the first two days of combat. The tribe of Benjamin comes very close to being obliterated. In the providence of God, a remnant of Benjamin is preserved so the first King of Israel and the greatest Missionary of all time will arrive in due time. If Benjamin had been wiped out there would have been no King Saul and no Paul the Apostle. Much of the unseen future was riding on this battle in the beginning of the days of the Judges.

Chapter 21

21.1-23 Now the men of Israel had sworn in Mizpeh, saying, There shall not any of us give his daughter unto Benjamin to wife. 2 And the people came to the house of God, and abode there till even before God, and lifted up their voices, and wept sore; 3 And said, O Lord God of Israel, why is this come to pass in Israel, that there should be to day one tribe lacking in Israel? 4 And it came to pass on the morrow, that the people rose early, and built there an altar, and offered burnt offerings and peace offerings. 5 And the children of Israel said, Who is there among all the tribes of Israel that came not up with the congregation unto the Lord? For they had made a great oath concerning him that came not up to the Lord to Mizpeh, saying, He shall surely be put to death. 6 And the children of Israel repented them for Benjamin their brother, and said, There is one tribe cut off from Israel this day. 7 How shall we do for wives for them that remain, seeing we have sworn by the Lord that we will not give them of our daughters to wives? 8 And they said, What one is there of the tribes of Israel that came not up to Mizpeh to the Lord? And, behold, there came none to the camp from Jabeshgilead to the assembly. 9 For the people were numbered, and, behold, there were none of the inhabitants of Jabeshgilead there. 10 And the congregation sent thither twelve thousand men of the valiantest, and commanded them, saying, Go and smite the inhabitants of Jabeshgilead with the edge of the sword, with the women and the children. 11 And this is the thing that ye shall do, Ye shall utterly destroy every male, and every woman that hath lain by man. 12 And they found among the inhabitants of Jabeshgilead four hundred young virgins, that had known no man by lying with any male: and they brought them unto the camp to Shiloh, which is in the land of Canaan. 13 And the whole congregation sent some to speak to the children of Benjamin that were in the rock Rimmon, and to call peaceably unto them. 14 And Benjamin came again at that time; and they gave them wives which they had saved alive of the women of Jabeshgilead: and yet so they sufficed them not. 15 And the people repented them for Benjamin, because that the Lord had made a breach in the tribes of Israel. 16 Then the elders of the congregation said, How shall we do for wives for them that remain, seeing the women are destroyed out of Benjamin? 17 And they said, There must be an inheritance for them that be escaped of Benjamin, that a tribe be not destroyed out of Israel. 18 Howbeit we may not give them wives of our daughters: for the children of Israel have sworn, saying, Cursed be he that giveth a wife to Benjamin. 19 Then they said, Behold, there is a feast of the Lord in Shiloh yearly in a place which is on the north side of Bethel, on the east side of the highway that goeth up from Bethel to Shechem, and on the south of Lebonah. 20 Therefore they commanded the children of Benjamin, saying, Go and lie in wait in the vineyards; 21 And see, and, behold, if the daughters of Shiloh come out to dance in dances, then come ye out of the vineyards, and catch you every man his wife of the daughters of Shiloh, and go to the land of Benjamin. 22 And it shall

be, when their fathers or their brethren come unto us to complain, that we will say unto them, Be favourable unto them for our sakes: because we reserved not to each man his wife in the war: for ye did not give unto them at this time, that ye should be guilty. 23 And the children of Benjamin did so, and took them wives, according to their number, of them that danced, whom they caught: and they went and returned unto their inheritance, and repaired the cities, and dwelt in them.

21.1-23 The preservation of Benjamin. Only the omnipotent God can maintain the balance of judgment and mercy. To judge this horrible sin yet maintain the mercy upon the tribe of Benjamin is truly a balancing act of God. We see here how He excels in it while guiding men through their own conscience to find a way to accomplish this balance. The bloodlust of Israel recedes quickly, and the result of the carnage is humbling. It appears even the women and children were massacred, for there are only 600 men left. It appears justice overshot the mark. One concubine-wife was killed in the beginning, and in return every married woman of Jabesh Gilead was slain. Only the virgins were spared. This provided wives for 400 men of Benjamin, but not all the men of this tribe. The solution they provided was to kidnap young women who danced at the celebration of the feast of Jehovah. This is probably the Feast of Tabernacles or the Passover. These young maidens were paying tribute to Miriam and the dance of victory at the Red Sea.

21.24-25 And the children of Israel departed thence at that time, every man to his tribe and to his family, and they went out from thence every man to his inheritance. 25 In those days there was no king in Israel: every man did that which was right in his own eyes.

21.24-25 Conclusion. It is difficult to sum up 450 years in a short concise paragraph. These leaders performed feats never equaled in world history. They were military leaders as well as civil leaders. Their personalities and accomplishments are quite diverse. They preserved the way of life given them by the first generation of emigrant Israelis. The history here recorded covers every section of the promised land. The story of Judges is footnoted and amended in the short book that follows, the book of Ruth. Judges gives us the view into human hearts without the leadership of God. This theme is bridged into the Book of Samuel where Samuel the last judge transitions into the Monarchy. Judges does not end as per se. It transitions into the next phase of Biblical history, the 450 years of kings and one queen. Was this period of time a success or failure? It was both. The success is the nation survived the wars of seven other nations stronger than they were. The nation is preserved. The failure is the sinister actions of man without leadership. This era of every man doing that which was right in his own eyes stand as a sentinel of warning to every future generation. Mankind must have leadership. Without God, mankind sinks to austere levels of inhumanity.

The Story Behind the Expository Series

This is a story about a man, his morals, and his ethics. The man's name was Millard Deramus. He was my paternal grandfather.

Millard lived at the end of a dirt and gravel road in Western Central Arkansas. When the road, as it was, reached his homestead, it turned and headed out of the woods. He was born a quarter of a mile from where he lived his entire life. I am not sure if he ever ventured out of the state of Arkansas. Possibly he got as far as a neighboring state once.

Many years ago he had a neighbor he simply referred to as Mr. Poole. One day Mr. Poole left. When it came time to pay the yearly taxes on their property, Mr. Poole had not returned. Millard was a good neighbor, so he did what he felt good neighbors do, he decided Mr. Poole's taxes should be paid so when Mr. Poole returned, he would not be in arrears with the state of Arkansas.

Millard hitched his mules and went on to Mr. Poole's land and cut a load of pulp wood and took it to the mill and sold it. He then went to the county seat and paid Mr. Poole's taxes. The next year Mr. Poole had still not returned, so Millard again cut pulp wood off Mr. Poole's land, sold it, and paid the taxes on Mr. Poole's land. This continued for many, many years. Mr. Poole never returned and each year my grandfather would cut timber off of Mr. Poole's land and sell it and pay the taxes on Mr. Poole's land.

I was there the day the attorney came to see Millard. We were on the back porch that had been screened in, and we were drinking coffee. I still have the two coffee cups we used that day. I heard the conversation from three feet away. The attorney had a briefcase full of papers he wanted Millard to sign.

The attorney informed Millard that according to the state of Arkansas, Millard was the owner of the 280 acres next door by the default of paying the taxes for the last 20 years. The name Millard Deramus was on every yearly receipt for over 20 years. The amount of money being discussed was substantial. I watched my grandfather closely. There was no reaction at all. No smile, not even a raised eyebrow.

Millard patiently waited for the attorney to finish. The attorney requested my grandfather sign the documents accepting ownership of 280 acres that joined his 70 acres. The value of the land at that time, including the timber, was well over a quarter of a million dollars. When the attorney finished and asked my grandfather to sign the documents he quietly and firmly said no, I will not sign. He informed the attorney that was not his land and he had never taken anything that did not belong to him in his life.

The amount of money was staggering to me. I was watching a man who had lived a simple rustic life for all of his eighty-plus years. He wore bib overalls and drove old pick-up trucks. When younger, he worked as a blacksmith out under the oak tree in his yard. I still have items he forged under that old oak tree. I watched that day as the attorney attempted to stoke the fire of avarice in Millard Deramus.

The attorney told Millard all he could do with several hundred thousand dollars. He floated the idea of a new home, a new truck, retirement, travel. Millard just stared at the attorney. No comment. None. The attorney tried again. Will you just sign, Millard? For your children? No comment. None. Finally the attorney asked, "Is there anything I can do to get you to sign these papers?" My grandfather simply shook his head no. He said one sentence. He said, "It ain't my land."

My grandfather died and was buried a short distance from where he lived his entire life. My grandmother (Dolly) lived a few more years. The children convinced her to sign the papers to claim ownership of the land because otherwise it would simply go back to the state. She signed, the land was sold, and my father was one of eight children who inherited.

When my father died I received my inheritance, part of which was the money from the sale of Mr. Poole's land. For a long time I pondered what to do. I did not feel like I could accept money I had witnessed my grandfather refuse on the afternoon on the back porch so many years before. So I waited. I did nothing. I never spent one dime of that money.

In 2016 an idea came to me that seemed an appropriate way to use that money. It is the money being used to produce the Expository Series. I did not know of any Apostolic writings that were doing an Expository Series. So I took that money and began to print books for Apostolic people to read.

The books of the Expository Series are printed without charge to the authors. The proceeds and profit of the books sold online go back into a non-profit fund to print more Apostolic books. None of the online profit is going to any personal use for anyone. If an author buys his book direct from wholesale after it is published and sells it, then he is welcomed to keep any profit from those sales.

I would like to thank all the men who have contributed their work to this endeavor. Scott Hall, Bart Adkins, Vaughn Reece, Kevin Archer, Ben Weeks, and Edward Seabrooks have all contributed. We have now published fifteen volumes and have three more to be published in the next sixty days. Others have also shown interest in publishing their works. Our goal is to have twenty volumes published by the end of 2017.

The publisher we are using has informed me we are their best seller they have ever published. We have now sold several thousand dollars of books since September 1, 2016. I am deeply grateful to everyone who has purchased our product.

Now you know the story behind the Expository Series. A simple Christian man with ethics and morals, opened his heart, and showed me his faith on a warm spring day, in a simple homestead, many years ago. Today I say thank you to my grandfather, Millard Deramus. Thank you for your ethics. Thank you for your morals. Thank you for your Christian faith.

May your memory be blessed and revered. You never travelled 100 miles from where you were born, but your legacy has spanned America.

www.ingramcontent.com/pod-product-compliance
Lightning Source LLC
Chambersburg PA
CBHW071741080526
44588CB00013B/2117